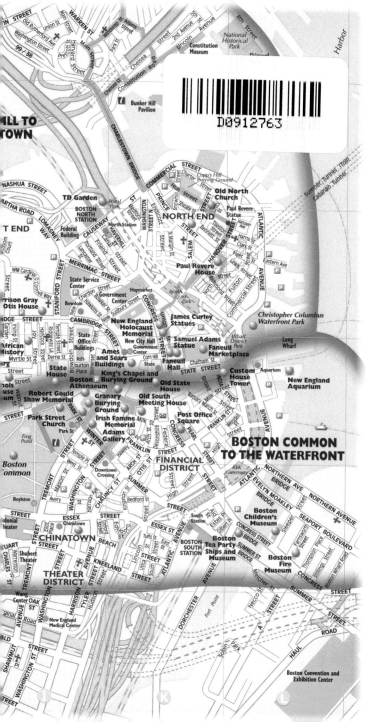

WARREN ST

Old Richmond Ave
Union St
Main St
Washington Street
99 / 38
Harvard
Pres
Common
Street
Chelsea
Park St
Chelsea Street
Constitution Road
2nd Avenue
Lincoln
Avenue
8th Street
Constitution
Museum
National
Historical
Park
Harbor

ILL TO
TOWN

Bunker Hill
Pavilion

CHARLESTOWN BRIDGE

COMMERCIAL STREET
Charter Street
Copp's Hill
Burying Ground
Old North
Church
Paul Revere
Statue

NASHUA STREET
TD Garden
BOSTON
NORTH
STATION
North Station
Portal
Park
WASHINGTON STREET
PRINCE STREET
SALEM STREET
Hanover Street
NORTH END
Summer Tunnel/Train
Callahan Tunnel

ARTHA ROAD
T END
LOMASNEY WAY
Federal Building
CAUSEWAY
Friend Street
Portland Street
Lancaster Street
MERRIMAC STREET
Cooper Street
Endicott Street
North
End
Park
Paul Revere
House
Bennett Street
Clark St
Harris St
Fleet
Fulton
North Street
Commercial Street
ATLANTIC AVENUE
Eastern Ave

WM Cardinal
O'Connell Way
STANIFORD STREET
State Service
Center
Chardon Street
Hawkins St
New Sudbury Street
Government
Center
Haymarket
CAMBRIDGE STREET
Union Street
Christopher Columbus
Waterfront Park
Wharf
District
Park
Long
Wharf

rison Gray
Otis House
IDGE STREET
African
History
rg
Bowdoin
Myrtle St
Derne St
State
Office
Buildings
New England
Holocaust
Memorial
New City Hall
Government
Center
Corn Hill
James Curley
Statues
Samuel Adams
Statue
Faneuil
Marketplace
STATE STREET
Custom
House
Tower
Aquarium
New England
Aquarium

State
Street
Ames
and Sears
Buildings
King's Chapel and
Burying Ground
Old State
House
Broad Street
India Street
Milk Street

State House
Bowdoin St
Ashburton Place
Boston
Athenaeum
Granary
Burying
Ground
Old South
Meeting House
Battery March Street
CONGRESS STREET
FRANKLIN STREET
P

Robert Gould
Shaw Memorial
Park Street
Church
Irish Famine
Memorial
Adams
Gallery
Post Office
Square
High Street
BOSTON COMMON
TO THE WATERFRONT

Frog
Pond
Park St
WINTER STREET
Temple Pl
West St
Milk St
Federal Street
Pearl Street

Boston
Common
Boylston
TREMONT STREET
Mason St
Avery
WASHINGTON STREET
Downtown
Crossing
ARCH ST
SUMMER STREET
OTIS STREET
Bedford St
Kingston Street
FINANCIAL
DISTRICT
RKB
Greenway
ATLANTIC AVENUE
NORTHERN AVE
EVELYN MOAKLEY
BRIDGE
NORTHERN AVENUE
SEAPORT BOULEVARD

STREET
Colonial
Theater
CHAUNCY ST
Harrison Avenue
ESSEX STREET
BEACH STREET
South
Station
BOSTON
SOUTH
STATION
SUMMER ST BRIDGE
CONGRESS ST BRIDGE
Boston
Children's
Museum
Sleeper Street
Farnsworth Street
Thomson Place

ESSEX
Chinatown
Edinboro St
Tufts St
East
Oak
Lincoln Street
ATLANTIC AVENUE
Boston
Tea Party
Ships and
Museum
Boston
Fire
Museum
Stillings Street
Boston Wharf Road

UART
CHARLES
Shubert Theater
TREMONT STREET
KNEELAND STREET
Utica St
Hudson Street
Necco
Court
Meicher St
SUMMER STREET

THEATER
DISTRICT
Wang
Center
OAK ST
WASHINGTON STREET
HARRISON AVENUE
TYLER ST
Hudson
DORCHESTER AVENUE
Fort Point
Sobin Park
CONGRESS STREET
A STREET
HAUL ROAD

CHINATOWN
New England
Medical Center
binal Road
SHAWMUT

LD
WASHINGTON ST
STREET
P
TREET

Boston Convention and
Exhibition Center

J
K
L

Fodor's
25 Best

BOSTON

How to Use
This Book

KEY TO SYMBOLS

✚ Map reference to the accompanying fold-out map

✉ Address

☎ Telephone number

🕐 Opening/closing times

🍴 Restaurant or café

🚉 Nearest rail station

Ⓜ Nearest subway (Metro) station

🚌 Nearest bus route

🚢 Nearest riverboat or ferry stop

♿ Facilities for visitors with disabilities

❷ Other practical information

▷ Further information

ℹ Tourist information

✋ Admission charges: Expensive (over $10), Moderate ($6–$10) and Inexpensive ($5 or less)

This guide is divided into four sections

• **Essential Boston:** An introduction to the city and tips on making the most of your stay.

• **Boston by Area:** We've broken the city into five areas, and recommended the best sights, shops, entertainment venues, nightlife and restaurants in each one. Suggested walks help you to explore on foot.

• **Where to Stay:** The best hotels, whether you're looking for luxury, budget or something in between.

• **Need to Know:** The info you need to make your trip run smoothly, including getting about by public transportation, weather tips, emergency phone numbers and useful websites.

Navigation In the Boston by Area chapter, we've given each area its own color, which is also used on the locator maps throughout the book and the map on the inside front cover.

Maps The fold-out map accompanying this book is a comprehensive street plan of Boston. The grid on this fold-out map is the same as the grid on the locator maps within the book. We've given grid references within the book for each sight and listing.

Contents

ESSENTIAL BOSTON   **4–18**

Introducing Boston	4–5
A Short Stay in Boston	6–7
Top 25	8–9
Shopping	10–11
Shopping by Theme	12
Boston by Night	13
Eating Out	14
Restaurants by Cuisine	15
Top Tips For…	16–18

BOSTON BY AREA   **19–106**
BEACON HILL TO
CHARLESTOWN   **20–46**

Area Map	22–23
Sights	24–39
Walk	40
Shopping	41–42
Entertainment and Nightlife	43
Restaurants	44–46

BOSTON COMMON TO
THE WATERFRONT   **47–62**

Area Map	48–49
Sights	50–56
Walk	57
Shopping	58
Entertainment and Nightlife	59–60
Restaurants	61–62

BACK BAY AND THE
SOUTH END   **63–84**

Area Map	64–65
Sights	66–78
Walk	79
Shopping	80–81
Entertainment and Nightlife	82–83
Restaurants	84

CAMBRIDGE   **85–98**

Area Map	86–87
Sights	88–92
Walk	93
Shopping	94–95
Entertainment and Nightlife	96–97
Restaurants	97–98

FARTHER AFIELD   **99–106**

Area Map	100–101
Sights	102–104
Excursions	105–106

WHERE TO STAY   **107–112**

Introduction	108
Budget Hotels	109
Mid-Range Hotels	110–111
Luxury Hotels	112

NEED TO KNOW   **113–125**

Planning Ahead	114–115
Getting There	116–117
Getting Around	118–119
Essential Facts	120–123
Timeline	124–125

CONTENTS

3

Introducing Boston

From its 17th-century beginnings as a British colony, Boston has been a town of undeniable independent spirit. Its plucky revolutionaries earned it that reputation early on, and the city itself has upheld the tradition ever since.

Massachusetts has led many of the country's most important movements—public education, the abolition of slavery, women's equality and gay rights. Boston and Cambridge, its sister city across the Charles River (in this book, references to Boston include Cambridge), have been at the forefront of these campaigns.

The city's dedication to culture and learning is well known, and can be seen in its world-class museums, concert halls and libraries, and in the countless college campuses. Even the music clubs, galleries and movie theaters have their own histories.

Meanwhile, Boston's quality of life is equally high out of doors. The string of parks and public spaces designed by Frederick Law Olmsted (collectively known as the "Emerald Necklace") runs through the city, providing stunning and well-maintained green space in many a neighborhood. Water is almost always nearby or visible, from the Charles River Esplanade of Back Bay to the downtown area bordering Boston Harbor. And Boston's architecture is some of the most beautiful in the country: as often as not, Victorian brownstones share blocks with art deco buildings and contemporary skyscrapers.

Of course, none of these perks comes cheap. Boston's real estate is some of the most expensive in the country, and is seemingly ever on the rise. That's largely because, unlike many American cities, it has made urban living desirable, so its residents are willing to spend what's necessary to live there. All in all, there are few cities in America more worth taking up residence in—or visiting.

Facts + Figures

- The "T" was the first subway system in the US. The first section opened in 1897.
- Boston Common was the first public park in America.
- Harvard University was the first college in North America.

ODD FACTS

- Some 58 percent of Boston is built on landfill.
- Boston Light, on Little Brewster Island, was the first lighthouse in the United States (1716). It is still in operation.
- The Boston University Bridge is the only place in the world where a boat can sail under a train driving under a car driving under a plane.

LOCAL PASSIONS

● Ice cream (they eat more of it in Boston than in any other city in the US).
● Baseball (traffic brings the area around Fenway Park to a halt for every game).
● Music (ranging from local bands to symphony orchestras).

GETTING YOUR BEARINGS

Boston Common and the Public Garden lie at the heart of Boston. To their north is the old residential area of Beacon Hill. Southeast of the Common are the Theater District and Chinatown. The Freedom Trail, which starts on the Common, runs northeast through Old Boston, past Faneuil Hall to the Italian North End. Across the Charles River lies Harvard Square in Cambridge.

A Short Stay in Boston

DAY 1

Morning On your way to the **New England Aquarium** (▷ 53) start at **Espresso Love** (▷ 61) at 8.30 for blueberry scones, muffins and coffee. When the Aquarium opens at 9, walk its corridors to see both exotic and local sealife.

Mid-morning Make your way to **Faneuil Hall and Marketplace** (▷ 26) perusing the artist carts and watching the street performers along the way. Then walk past City Hall on to Tremont Street, and take a right on Beacon Street for a walk over historic **Beacon Hill** (▷ 24–25). After admiring the gold-domed **State House** (▷ 35), pass behind it down Mount Vernon Street, and take in upscale **Louisburg Square** (▷ 24–25) and quaint, cobbled Acorn Street.

Lunch At the bottom of the hill, take a right on **Charles Street** (▷ 42). Stop at **Artù** (▷ 45) at 89 Charles Street for a panini, salad or pizza.

Afternoon Visit the antiques shops on Charles Street or visit **Nichols House** (▷ 39) or the **Museum of African American History** (▷ 39).

Mid-afternoon Continue to the end of Charles Street, past the T station to the **Liberty Hotel** (▷ 112) for a drink in the Liberty Lobby bar, and to admire the stunning architectural transformation of this former city jail.

Dinner Return to Charles Street for dinner at the **Beacon Hill Bistro** (▷ 45) or at the nearby **Upper Crust Pizzeria** (▷ 46) for authentic Italian pizzas.

Evening Take a 10-minute walk through **Boston Common** or the **Public Garden** (▷ 50), or a five-minute taxi ride around it, to the Theater District, to see a play in any of the city's excellent theaters.

DAY 2

Morning Start the day with a Parisian or American breakfast at **Brasserie JO** (▷ 84), opposite the Prudential Center, and continue along Huntington Avenue past Symphony Hall to the **Museum of Fine Arts** (▷ 70). It's easy to spend a day among its vast collections of French Impressionists, Egyptian artifacts and Early American decorative arts.

Mid-morning Walk along the Fens to the Isabella Stewart Gardner Museum (▷ 68–69) for a look at the home of a Boston legend and a stroll through her fabulous art collection.

Lunch Take the T to Harvard Square for lunch at **Tory Row** (▷ 98), a few steps from the station. Tory was the nickname for a British loyalist at the time of the Revolution, but today's menu is strictly modern American.

Afternoon Cross Harvard Yard to see the one-of-a-kind collection of glass flowers at the **Harvard Museum of Natural History** and a look at the Native American collections at the adjoining **Peabody Museum** (▷ 91).

Mid-afternoon Take a break from museums at **L. A. Burdick Chocolate Shop & Café** (▷ 98) before continuing down Brattle Street for a look at the **Longfellow House** (▷ 92).

Dinner Choose between two of Cambridge's most sophisticated restaurants. Chef Jason Bond's **Bondir** (▷ 97) is tiny, but his contemporary New England dishes are a revelation. Or head for **Oleana** (▷ 98), where chef Ana Sortun focuses on subtly spiced Eastern Mediterranean food: bay scallops with orange-saffron broth, crispy duck with Persian black-eyed peas. Otherwise, dine at **Sandrine's** (▷ 98), and enjoy the Alsatian chef/owner's blend of French styles and seasonal local ingredients.

Top 25

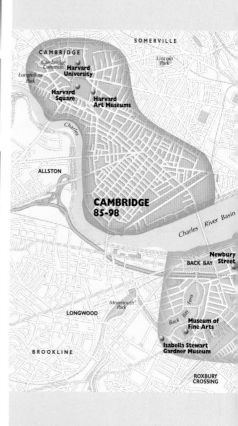

►►►

Beacon Hill and Louisburg Square ▷ 24–25
Elegant residential district with some historic homes.

USS *Constitution* and Charlestown ▷ 36–37
Naval museums and historic warships.

Trinity Church and Copley Square ▷ 76–77 New (John Hancock Tower) and old (Trinity Church) architecture rub shoulders in this square.

State House ▷ 35
The gold-domed landmark center of state government.

The South End ▷ 74–75
Lively, sought-after residential area with excellent restaurants and shops.

Prudential Center and Skywalk ▷ 73 An upscale shopping mall and stunning panoramic views from the 50th floor.

Paul Revere House ▷ 34 The legendary revolutionary's North End home and one of the few houses left from colonial America.

Boston Common and Public Garden ▷ 50
Open-air playgrounds, ponds and gardens.

Boston Harbor Islands ▷ 102 Unspoiled havens of wildlife, historic forts and beaches.

Old State House ▷ 32–33 Best museum for an overview of Boston's rich history.

North End and Old North Church ▷ 30–31 Historic church in the heart of Little Italy.

Newbury Street ▷ 72
Funky shops, luxury boutiques, pavement cafés and trendy restaurants.

ESSENTIAL BOSTON TOP 25

8

These pages are a quick guide to the Top 25, which are described in more detail later. Here they are listed alphabetically, and the tinted background shows which area they are in.

Boston Public Library
▷ **66** Marbles, mosaics and murals in an oasis of tranquillity.

Boston Tea Party Ships & Museum ▷ **51** Get the facts about the events of December 16, 1773.

Commonwealth Avenue ▼▼▼
▷ **67** Boston's grandest houses flank a green mall with noted statues.

Faneuil Hall and Marketplace ▷ **26** From first public meeting hall to food market and mall.

Harrison Gray Otis House ▷ **27** Restored Federal-style family home.

Harvard Square and Harvard University ▷ **88–89** Cafés, shops, street entertainers—the hub of student life.

Harvard University and Art Museums ▷ **90–91** World-quality museums.

Institute of Contemporary Art ▷ **52** Cutting-edge architecture on the waterfront.

Isabella Stewart Gardner Museum ▷ **68–69** Superb works of art displayed in a palazzo setting.

JFK Library and Museum ▷ **103** Insight into JFK's life. His papers are held here.

BEACON HILL TO CHARLESTOWN 20–46

CHARLESTOWN
Bunker Hill Monument
National Historical Park
USS Constitution

Museum of Science
Charles River Dam
EAST CAMBRIDGE
WEST END
NORTH END
Old North Church
Christopher Columbus Waterfront Park
Charlesbank Park
Paul Revere House
Boston Inner Harbor

Harrison Gray Otis House
Faneuil Marketplace
Boston Harbor Islands

BEACON HILL
State House
Louisburg Square
Esplanade
Old State House
Faneuil Hall
New England Aquarium

Public Garden
Boston Common
FINANCIAL DISTRICT
Institute of Contemporary Art
Commonwealth Avenue
Prudential Center
Trinity Church and Copley Square
CHINATOWN
Boston Tea Party Ships and Museum
Boston Public Library
THEATER DISTRICT
BOSTON COMMON TO THE WATERFRONT 47–62
Prudential Skywalk

SOUTH END
BACK BAY AND THE SOUTH END 63–84
SOUTH BOSTON
JFK Library and Museum

New England Aquarium ▷ **53** A large collection— families will love this. Don't miss feeding time.

Museum of Science ▷ **28–29** Cutting-edge exhibits cover ocean waves to space travel.

Museum of Fine Arts ▷ **70–71** An exhaustive collection of treasures from around the globe.

◀◀◀

Shopping

Some of Boston's best shopping areas are in the city's most attractive neighborhoods. One-of-a-kind shops selling clothes, books or antiques rub shoulders with outlets for contemporary crafts, innovative gifts and home accessories. Newbury Street is a joy, with its boutiques in lovely 19th-century brownstone buildings. People travel long distances to shop for clothes here, from top designer labels to the fabulously funky and the "gently used." With the great outdoors on the doorstep, many shops specialize in outdoors equipment and clothing.

Antiques

Like all of New England, Boston is good hunting ground for antiques. Clustered in and around Charles Street, at the foot of Beacon Hill, are dozens of shops. Most are specialists, selling oriental rugs, furniture, porcelain, silver or antique maps for serious money. Even if you can't afford to buy, it's a pleasure to browse. In Cambridge, hundreds of dealers in two large markets offer less expensive collectibles, alongside furniture, silverware and other antiques.

Books

Boston has a plethora of bookshops—new, used and antiquarian—particularly around Harvard Square. Whether you're looking for a coffee-table book on Boston to take back home, or something rare and erudite, you can browse undisturbed until 11pm in some stores.

ONLY IN BOSTON

Baked beans were invented in Boston by early colonists, who cooked them in molasses. Today, red Boston beans (albeit in candy form) are sold on souvenir stands. The lobster shows up in the usual touristy guises, from fridge magnets to pencil tops and notebooks. As for T-shirts, sweatshirts and baseball caps, they bear logos of local universities, like Harvard, and local pro teams, including the Patriots, the Bruins, the Celtics and, of course, the 2004, 2007 and 2013 World Series winners, the Red Sox.

Clockwise from top left: Downtown Crossing; colorful handmade glass; shop sign; Harvard

Boutiques

Many of the small independent stores in Back Bay, Beacon Hill, the South End and Cambridge brim with interesting finds—from pottery made by Boston artists and soaps made by local beauty companies to hand-knit sweaters. Even on Newbury Street, which at first glance seems to be full of pricey international brands, you'll find local businesses tucked in among the heavy hitters.

Outlet Shopping

A massive housing, office and restaurant development in the suburb of Somerville revolves around the outlets at Assembly Row (▷ 95). Only minutes from downtown on the T are 50 outlet stores, offering discounts of up to 65 percent on clothing, shoes, sports gear and more.

Farmers' Markets

At the farmers' markets that start up in spring in Copley Square (Tuesday, Friday), South Station (Tuesday, Thursday) and Harvard Square (Tuesday), you can find all the goodies available at roadside farm stands around rural areas of New England—fresh fruits, ice cream, maple syrup, cheese and honey, among other things. Maple-cream candy and plastic jugs of maple syrup make easy-to-pack souvenirs and gifts.

Contemporary Crafts

The best (and easy-to-find) places to shop for contemporary crafts are in Newbury and Charles streets, as well as in Cambridge and the South End.

Book Store; Faneuil Hall Marketplace; shop sign in Beacon Hill

UNIQUELY BOSTON

Shopping is one of the favorite activities for visitors to Boston, with some tourism surveys ranking shopping popularity higher than visiting the museums and historic attractions. Clothing costing less than $175 is exempt from the 6.25 percent Massachusetts sales tax. Good shopping areas are located in Back Bay and South End, Beacon Hill and Faneuil Hall, Downtown and Cambridge.

Shopping by Theme

You'll find all sorts of shops in Boston. On this page they are listed by theme with cross references to more detailed information.

ANTIQUES

Cambridge Antique Market (▷ 94)
Charles Street (▷ panel, 42)
Danish Country Antiques (▷ 41)

BOOKS AND MAPS

Brattle Book Shop (▷ 58)
Grolier Poetry Bookshop (▷ 94)
Harvard Book Store (▷ 94)
Harvard Coop (▷ 94)
Schoenhof's Foreign Books (▷ 94)
The World's Only Curious George Store (▷ 95)

FOR CHILDREN

Build-A-Bear Workshop (▷ 41)
The Red Wagon (▷ 42)
Stellabella Toys (▷ 95)
The World's Only Curious George Store (▷ 95)

CLOTHES AND ACCESSORIES

Alan Bilzerian (▷ 80)
American Apparel (▷ 80)
Coach (▷ 41)
Crush Boutique (▷ 80)
Emporio Armani (▷ 80)
Flock Boutique (▷ 80)
Goorin Bros (▷ 81)
Holiday Boutique (▷ 42)
Linens on the Hill (▷ 42)
Looks (▷ 95)
LouisBoston (▷ 58)
Marc Jacobs (▷ 81)
Mint Julep (▷ 95)
Nomad (▷ 95)
St. John Boutique (▷ 58)
Second Time Around (▷ 81)
Tess & Carlos (▷ 95)
Urban Outfitters (▷ 95)
Wish Boutique (▷ 42)

CRAFTS

Bead + Fiber (▷ 80)
Boston Bead Company (▷ 94)
Cambridge Artists' Cooperative (▷ 94)

DISTRICTS AND MALLS

Assembly Row (▷ panel, 95)
Barneys New York (▷ 80)
CambridgeSide Galleria (▷ 41)
Charles Street (▷ panel, 42)
Downtown Crossing (▷ 58)
Harvard Square (▷ 94)
Newbury Street (▷ panel, 81)
Prudential Center (▷ 81)

FOODS

Beacon Hill Chocolates (▷ 41)
Cardullo's (▷ 94)
Hidden Sweets (▷ 94)
Savenor's (▷ 42)

GIFTS/HOUSEHOLD

Abodeon (▷ 94)
Black Ink (▷ 41)
Boston Pewter Company (▷ 41)
Bostonian Society Museum Shop (▷ 41)
Bromfield Pen Shop (▷ 58)
Brookstone (▷ 80)
Coco Baby (▷ 80)
Eugene Galleries (▷ 41)
Flat of the Hill (▷ 42)
Geoclassics (▷ 42)
Gifted (▷ 80)
Good, Inc (▷ 42)
The ICA Store (▷ 58)
Joie de Vivre (▷ 95)
Leavitt & Peirce Inc. (▷ 95)
Lekker (▷ 81)
Life is Good (▷ 81)
Lush (▷ 81)
noa (▷ 42)
Officina 189 (▷ 42)
Period Furniture Hardware Co. (▷ 42)
Simon Pearce (▷ 81)
Williams-Sonoma (▷ 81)

MUSIC

Newbury Comics (▷ 81, 95)

OUTDOOR GEAR

Allen Edmonds (▷ 80)
Foot Paths (▷ 58)
Hilton's Tent City (▷ 42)
Niketown (▷ 81)
Skechers (▷ 58)
The Tannery (▷ 58)

Boston by Night

Although Boston's not a city that never sleeps, you'll still find evening diversions aplenty.

Illuminations
For magical views of Boston's skyline visit the Prudential Skywalk, or cross over the Charles River to Cambridge on the T. Memorial Drive, between Longfellow and Harvard bridges, is a good spot to view the floodlit downtown skyscrapers. In winter, trees twinkle with lights.

People-Watching
One of the liveliest spots for people-watching is the North End, where Italian music fills the narrow streets and restaurants hum with the chatter of Italian families. On Newbury Street people sit outdoors in cafés surveying the pedestrian parade.

Clubs and Bars
Boston club kids head for Lansdowne Street, near Kenmore Square. For cocktails and to catch the latest music, young professionals go to Boylston Place, a little alley in the Theater District. The Regattabar (▷ 96) on Harvard Square is one of the best-known jazz venues on the East Coast.

Late-Night Restaurants
Most restaurants do not serve after midnight, but you could try Chinatown, where many places stay open until 4am. In the South End, several restaurants serve until 1am on weekends.

From top: Faneuil Hall; Fenway Park; Chinatown; nightclub; Hatch Shell

LIVE ENTERTAINMENT

Entertainment ranges from the Boston Symphony, Boston Ballet and traveling Broadway shows to rock concerts, avant-garde dance and student theater. In summer, see free movies, concerts and theater on outdoor stages. There are summer concerts at Hatch Shell (▷ 83), as well as free movies. Watch for free band concerts on City Hall Plaza (☎ 617/635-4505) in July and August, and for performances by Boston Landmarks Orchestra (☎ 617/987-2000; www.landmarksorchestra.org).

Eating Out

Once known primarily as the home of beans and cod, Boston has blossomed into a first-rate culinary center.

Eclectic Menus

Boston's restaurants are some of the country's best, from the snazzy bar-restaurants of Back Bay to its four-star New American ones. Where fried seafood and traditional Yankee fare once dominated menus, they're now offered alongside local seafood, with mignonette-splashed oysters and ceviche appearing regularly.

Bistros

In general, bistros are the most popular genre of restaurant around town; they tend to show up as hip, candlelit spots on Newbury Street or family-run joints in the South End. What they have in common is a sophisticated but unpretentious quality, and often excellent food.

Elegant Dining

A level or two up in price and service, you'll find sophisticated dishes made by Boston's most admired chefs, many of whom have been in the city for years.

Ethnic Restaurants

Boston's ethnic cuisines go beyond Chinatown and the North End Italian neighborhood. In Cambridge, the Portuguese enclave is around Inman Square, and several Irish pubs are nearby. Elsewhere in the city are Ethiopian, Asian and Latin American restaurants.

OPENING TIMES

Restaurant times vary slightly all over the city, but most open for dinner at 5 or 6pm and many serve dinner until 11pm or midnight, and offer an abridged menu if they happen to house a bar. Many of the trendier restaurants do not serve breakfast or lunch, and some are not open at all on Monday. Reservations are a must at any but the most casual places, but particularly at popular eating destinations like Back Bay and the South End.

From top: Newbury Street café; Faneuil Hall Marketplace; outdoor dining; Chinatown

Restaurants by Cuisine

There are restaurants to suit all tastes and budgets in Boston. On this page they are listed by cuisine. For a more detailed description of each restaurant, see Boston by Area.

AMERICAN AND MEXICAN

Anthem Kitchen + Bar (▷ 45)
Border Café (▷ 97)
The Butcher Shop (▷ 84)
Café Fleuri (▷ 61)
Craigie on Main (▷ 98)
Grill 23 & Bar (▷ 62)
Hungry I (▷ 45)
Mr. Bartley's Burger Cottage (▷ 98)
Paramount (▷ 46)
Union Bar & Grille (▷ 84)

ASIAN AND MIDDLE EASTERN

Chau Chow City (▷ 61)
Falafel King (▷ 45)
Haru (▷ 84)
Lala Rokh (▷ 46)
New Shanghai (▷ 62)

BOSTON'S BEST

Aura (▷ 61)
Bondir (▷ 97)
The Bristol Lounge (▷ 61)
Clio (▷ 84)
Durgin Park (▷ 45)
L'Espalier (▷ 84)
Hamersley's Bistro (▷ 84)
Marliave (▷ 62)
Meritage (▷ 62)
No. 9 Park (▷ 46)
Oleana (▷ 98)
Park (▷ 98)
Union Oyster House (▷ 46)

BRUNCH

The Blue Room (▷ 97)
Henrietta's Table (▷ panel, 98)

COFFEE AND SNACKS

Caffè Vittoria (▷ 45)
Christina's (▷ 97)
Espresso Love (▷ 61)
Flour Bakery (▷ panel, 84)
Hi-Rise (▷ 98)
L. A. Burdick Chocolate (▷ 98)
Maria's Pastry Shop (▷ 46)

FRENCH, ITALIAN AND MEDITERRANEAN

Antico Forno (▷ 45)
Artù (▷ 45)
Beacon Hill Bistro (▷ 45)
Bistro du Midi (▷ 61)
Brasserie Jo (▷ 84)
Cantina Italiana (▷ 45)
Casa Romero (▷ 84)
La Famiglia Giorgio's Restaurant (▷ 45)
Mamma Maria (▷ 46)

Petit Robert Bistro (▷ 84)
Prezza (▷ 46)
Rialto (▷ 98)
Sandrine's (▷ 98)
Teatro (▷ 62)
Upper Crust Pizzeria (▷ 46)
Via Matta (▷ 62)

SEAFOOD

Barking Crab (▷ 61)
Legal Sea Foods (▷ 98)
LTK Bar and Kitchen (▷ 62)
Neptune Oyster (▷ 46)
New Jumbo Seafood (▷ 62)
Rowes Wharf Sea Grille (▷ 62)

VEGETARIAN

Milk Street Café (▷ panel, 62)
My Thai Vegan Café (▷ panel, 62)
Tory Row (▷ 98)

Top Tips For…

However you'd like to spend your time in Boston, these top suggestions should help you tailor your ideal visit. Each suggestion has a fuller write-up elsewhere in the book.

LAZY MORNINGS

Take a stroll through the Public Garden (▷ 50).
Sip a coffee and people-watch from a table outside Maria's Pastry Shop (▷ 46) in the North End.
Walk along the Charles River Esplanade, the scenic pathway stretching along the river (▷ 78).
Go whale-watching out of Boston Harbor from the Aquarium (▷ 53).

SPECIALIST SHOPPING

Find the perfect shirt at a Newbury Street boutique (▷ 72).
Dig into some of the city's hottest music at Newbury Comics (▷ 81).
Act wonderfully childishly at The World's Only Curious George Store (▷ 95).
Find one-of-a-kind crafts and handmade jewelry at the ICA Store (▷ 58).
Discover new specialty cheeses and meats at Savenor's Market (▷ 42).

The swan boats in Boston Public Garden and trees on Charles River Esplanade (above)

BOSTON CULTURE

At Isabella Stewart Gardner Museum (▷ 68) see the stunning collection of international art in an attractive mansion.
View world-class collections at the Museum of Fine Arts (▷ 70): European and American art; Egyptian, Chinese and Classical artifacts.
Visit Trinity Church (▷ 76): A classic of Richardson Romanesque.
Listen to the renowned Boston Symphony Orchestra at Symphony Hall (▷ 83).

The neo-Romanesque Trinity Church reflected in the I. M. Pei-designed John Hancock Tower (above right); Boston Symphony Orchestra performing in Symphony Hall (right)

Spectacular view of Boston at night (below)

SKYSCRAPERS

Explore Prudential Tower (▷ 73): Ride up to the 50th-floor Skywalk.
Admire the John Hancock Tower (▷ 77): I. M. Pei & Partners designed this glass-enclosed building, which reflects the buildings surrounding it.
Ascend Custom House Tower (▷ 38) for the great views from this skyscraper-turned-hotel.

COMMUNING WITH NATURE

Relax in the Public Garden (▷ 50). Manicured and bustling, it's filled with citydwellers and tourists alike.
Amble through Back Bay Fens (▷ 78): A string of parks, once a shallow bay.
Watch the boats go by in Christopher Columbus Waterfront Park (▷ 38).
Experience the 281 acres (114ha) of lilac blooms, roses and rare Asian trees at Arnold Arboretum (▷ 104) in Cambridge.

White swan in the Public Garden (above middle); Arnold Arboretum (above)

A STATUE TRAIL

See a dramatic ode to the first all-black regiment to fight in the Civil War (▷ 56): Robert Gould Shaw Memorial facing the State House.
Make Way for the Ducklings: A charming tribute to Robert McCloskey's children's book, located in the Public Garden (▷ 50).
Honor three women who contributed to Boston's history—Abigail Adams, Lucy Stone and Phillis Wheatley at the Boston Women's Memorial on Commonwealth Avenue (▷ 67).

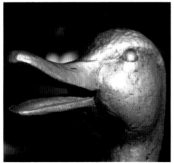

Bronze statue in the Public Garden (left), part of the collection inspired by Robert McCloskey's children's story "Make Way for Ducklings"

The Boston Children's Museum (below); the Museum of Fine Arts (below middle)

KEEPING THE CHILDREN OCCUPIED

Enjoy a fun, hands-on day of learning at the Museum of Science (▷ 28).
Find interactive exhibits on bubble-making, how televisions work and more at the Boston Children's Museum (▷ 54).
Take a dramatic, spiral trip around a glowing tank full of sea creatures at the New England Aquarium (▷ 53).

BEING ENTERTAINED

Get in on the act: American Repertory Theatre (▷ 96) is Harvard's innovative and ambitious production house.
Watch a highly regarded company performing classical and contemporary productions at José Mateo's Ballet Theatre (▷ 96).

LOOKING FOR A BARGAIN

Visit Harvard's three art museums Uniting the Fogg, Busch-Reisinger and Arthur M. Sackler museums is architect Renzo Piano's glass roof (▷ 91).
At the Museum of Fine Arts, pay what you like for entry on Wednesday nights after 4pm (▷ 70).
Find half-price theater tickets the day of a performance at BosTix booths (▷ panel, 59) at Faneuil Hall Marketplace and Copley Square.

The 18th-century Faneuil Hall (above)

ENJOYING NEW ENGLAND SEAFOOD

Head to Legal Sea Foods, (▷ 98) a locally based chain known for fresh lobsters and clam chowder.
Be more daring and head for LTK Bar and Kitchen (▷ 62) for international takes on the freshest seafood.

A seafood platter (right)

Boston by Area

Sights	24–39
Walk	40
Shopping	41–42
Entertainment and Nightlife	43
Restaurants	44–46

BEACON HILL TO CHARLESTOWN

Sights	50–56
Walk	57
Shopping	58
Entertainment and Nightlife	59–60
Restaurants	61–62

BOSTON COMMON TO THE WATERFRONT

Sights	66–78
Walk	79
Shopping	80–81
Entertainment and Nightlife	82–83
Restaurants	84

BACK BAY AND THE SOUTH END

Sights	88–92
Walk	93
Shopping	94–95
Entertainment and Nightlife	96–97
Restaurants	97–98

CAMBRIDGE

Sights	102–104
Excursions	105–106

FARTHER AFIELD

This neighborhood merges historic buildings and monuments with skyscrapers.

Sights	24–39
Walk	40
Shopping	41–42
Entertainment and Nightlife	43
Restaurants	45–46

Top 25 **TOP 25**

Beacon Hill and Louisburg Square ▷ **24**
Faneuil Hall and Marketplace ▷ **26**
Harrison Gray Otis House ▷ **27**
Museum of Science ▷ **28**
North End and Old North Church ▷ **30**
Old State House ▷ **32**
Paul Revere House ▷ **34**
State House ▷ **35**
USS *Constitution* and Charlestown ▷ **36**

Beacon Hill to Charlestown

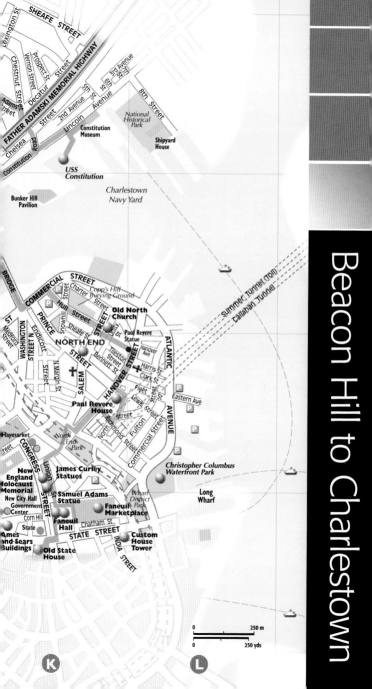

SHEAFE STREET

Chestnut Street

Prospect St

Vernon Street

Adams Street

Decatur Street

FATHER ADAMSKI MEMORIAL HIGHWAY

Chelsea Road

2nd Avenue

Lincoln Avenue

3rd Avenue

5th Avenue

8th Street

Constitution

National Historical Park

Constitution Museum

Shipyard House

USS Constitution

Charlestown Navy Yard

Bunker Hill Pavilion

BRIDGE

ST

Medford Street

COMMERCIAL STREET

Hull Street

Charter Street

Snowhill Street

Copp's Hill Burying Ground

PRINCE STREET

WASHINGTON STREET

Endicott Street

NORTH END

N Margin Street

SALEM STREET

HANOVER STREET

Sheafe Street

Tileston Street

Unity St

Old North Church

Paul Revere Statue

Bennett Street

Hanover Ave

ATLANTIC

Harris St

Clark St

Summer Tunnel (Toll)

Callahan Tunnel

Paul Revere House

Prince Street

North Margin Street

Fleet St

North Street

Lewis Street

Richmond Street

Fulton Street

Salem Street

Commercial Street

AVENUE

Eastern Ave

Haymarket

CONGRESS

Union Street

North End Park

New England Holocaust Memorial

New City Hall

Government Center

James Curley Statues

Samuel Adams Statue

STREET

Wharf District Park

Christopher Columbus Waterfront Park

Long Wharf

Corn Hill

Faneuil Hall

State

Chatham St

Faneuil Marketplace

Ames and Sears Buildings

Old State House

STATE STREET

INDIA STREET

Custom House Tower

0   250 m
0   250 yds

K   L

Beacon Hill to Charlestown

Beacon Hill and Louisburg Square

TOP
25

DE LUCA'S MARKET

FRESHEST BY FAR SINCE 1905

HIGHLIGHTS

- Louisburg Square
- Pinckney Street and its view of Charles River
- Nichols House Museum
- Charles Street shops and restaurants

BOSTON BRAHMINS

- Oliver Wendell Holmes called those Bostonians who could trace their origins to the wealthy merchants of the 18th and 19th centuries, Brahmins after the high-ranking Hindu caste.

Beacon Hill is an enclave of elegant redbrick houses in a leafy maze of steep streets and narrow, cobbled lanes—it is a delightful area to explore on foot.

Brahmin stronghold After the opening of the State House on its southern slope, Beacon Hill was developed as a prestigious residential area by entrepreneurs including Boston's famous architect Charles Bulfinch. Boston's top families swiftly moved in. Rich as they were, these "Brahmins" were also the personification of Puritan reserve. Showiness was taboo, so the houses were restrained, with elegant doorways and ironwork gracing plain brick facades.

Perfectly preserved To get the magic of it all, choose a sunny day and just wander, noting the

Clockwise from left: Mount Vernon Street; leafy Louisburg Square; cobbled Acorn Street in Beacon Hill; a redbrick building in the Beacon Hill district; autumn leaves; De Luca's Market on Charles Street

pillared porticoes, genteel fanlights and flowery window boxes. A walk through Beacon Hill leads you to some of the city's most treasured corners, including Mount Vernon Street, Chestnut Street, tiny Acorn Street and, best of all, Louisburg Square. Here Bulfinch's lovely bow fronts look onto a central garden reminiscent of a European square. Notice how the street lamps are lighted all day and look for the purple window panes: Manganese oxide in a batch of glass reacted with sunlight to produce discolored but now highly prized and very distinctive panes. To see inside a Beacon Hill home, visit the Nichols House Museum. On the hill's north slope from Pinckney Street down to Cambridge Street, the houses are smaller and more varied. It has several important sites in the history of Boston's African-American community, including the African Meeting House.

THE BASICS

✚ H5

✉ Bounded by Beacon Street, Embankment Road, Cambridge Street, Bowdoin Street

🍴 Choice in Charles Street

🚇 Park Street, Charles/ MGH, Arlington, Bowdoin (closed Sat)

♿ Steep hills, some uneven surfaces

❓ Historic New England tours of Beacon Hill; Black Heritage Trail: See Museum of African American History (▷ 39)

Faneuil Hall and Marketplace

A statue and an avenue of trees in front of Faneuil Hall (left); market stand (right)

THE BASICS

www.faneuilhallmarket place.com

⊕ K5

✉ Congress Street

☎ 617/242-5642

🕓 Great Hall: 9–5 (when not in use)

🍴 A plethora of eating places nearby

Ⓣ State, Aquarium, Government Center

♿ Good

✋ Great Hall: free

❓ Great Hall: 15-min talk every half hour

HIGHLIGHTS

● Great Hall
● Grasshopper weathervane on the roof
● Quincy's granite market buildings
● Street entertainers
● Food vendors in Quincy Market

Faneuil Hall is a landmark for all Americans, the place where the iniquities of the British government were first debated in the 1770s. Now, its marketplace is a landmark for visitors.

"Cradle of Liberty" A wealthy trader of Huguenot origins, Peter Faneuil presented the town with a market hall with a meeting room above. Ever since, the lower hall has been a market and the galleried upper hall has been a place for public gatherings. In the 1700s, because the town meetings frequently discussed the problems with Britain that led up to the revolution and independence, Faneuil Hall became known as America's "Cradle of Liberty." Since then national issues, from the abolition of slavery to the Vietnam War, have been aired here. The room bears all the trademarks of Charles Bulfinch, the architect who built so much of Boston. He expanded the hall in 1805.

Quincy's marketplace Despite the expansion, more space was needed. In 1826, with some inspired town planning that radically changed Boston's waterfront, mayor Josiah Quincy filled in Town Dock and built over the wharves, providing a granite market hall flanked by granite warehouses. These were a wholesale food market until the 1960s. In the 1970s the area was renovated and revitalized, and is now the city's main tourist attraction (known as Faneuil Hall Marketplace or Quincy Market) with shops, pushcarts, eating places and street entertainers.

The elegant dining room (right) of Harrison Gray Otis House (left)

This is a fine example of Federal-style architecture (1780–1830). Meticulously restored in every detail, the interior is an accurate representation of how the upper classes lived in the 19th century.

Otis and Bulfinch One of the leading lights in post-Revolutionary Boston politics was the lawyer Harrison Gray Otis (1765–1844), long-standing friend of architect Charles Bulfinch. In 1796 he commissioned Bulfinch to build him this grand mansion in what was then the elegant area of Bowdoin Square. The structure's very restrained, very proper, brick facade is typical of what became known as the Federal style. Five years later, Bulfinch built Otis an even bigger house on newly developed Beacon Hill (▷ 24–25). By the 1830s the Otis home had become a boarding house.

Authenticity In 1916 the Society for the Preservation of New England Antiquities, now Historic New England, bought the property as its headquarters. Accuracy and authenticity being its hallmarks, the organization has restored the interior with reproduction wallpapers and paint colors based on paint analysis. Otis and his wife, Sally, were lavish entertainers and the parlor, dining room and drawing room, furnished in high Federal style, provide an insight into social manners of the day, while bedrooms, kitchens and servant quarters give you a glimpse of family life. One upstairs room shows the mansion as it looked when it was a boarding house.

THE BASICS

www.historicnewengland.org

✚ J4

✉ 141 Cambridge Street

☎ 617/994-5920

🕐 Wed–Sun 11–5. Tours on the hour and half hour

🍴 None

Ⓟ Bowdoin (closed weekends), Charles/MGH, Government Center

♿ Wheelchairs first floor only

💵 Moderate. Historic New England members free

❓ Walking tours of Beacon Hill mid-May to mid-Oct, Sat (call ahead). Shop

HIGHLIGHTS

● Bulfinch Federal design
● Reproductions of original wallpaper
● Yellow and turquoise paints
● Federal-era furniture

Museum of Science

HIGHLIGHTS

● Lightning demo
● Full-motion simulator
● Natural Mysteries
● Mugar Omni Theater shows

TIPS

● Tickets for special exhibits often sell out during school vacation weeks. Buy in advance online.
● Arrive at least a half hour early for Mugar Omni Theater shows to get the best seats.

This place buzzes and hums with excited children running around pressing buttons and peering into things. There are hundreds of interactive exhibits, as well as live presentations.

Science now The museum prides itself on being at the cutting edge of science education. The museum complex straddles the Charles River, with views of the Cambridge and Boston skylines.

"It's awesome" Don't miss the dramatic indoor lightning demos in the Theater of Electricity, where the world's largest Van de Graaff generator creates 2.5 million volts of electricity. Between shows, take part in the popular Hands-On Laboratory. Close by, peer into the mouth of a T-Rex. A large portion of

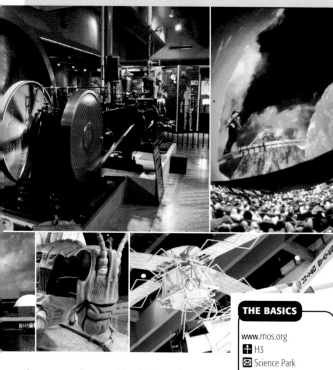

Clockwise from far left: A father and son examine an exhibit at the museum; the blur of the fast-spinning wheels of a steam-powered engine; a crowded show in the Mugar Omni Theater; a model space station; a giant locust model; the museum from the outside reflected in the Charles River

the museum has special exhibits, such as the free-flying Butterfly Garden, or cutting-edge 3D films about the human body. The Simulator Experience is a full-motion simulator excursion that takes you through space, the deep sea and along the path of a water molecule. Other exhibits include the Natural Mysteries, where you learn about scientific classification from skulls, animal tracks, shells and more. There are also presentations at the Science Live! Stage.

Mugar Omni Theater and the Planetarium

Lie back and be enveloped in the sight and sound of an IMAX movie in the five-story screen of the Mugar Omni Theater. Multimedia presentations at the Charles Hayden Planetarium cover astronomical subjects. Evening laser shows also take place here.

THE BASICS

www.mos.org

➕ H3

✉ Science Park

☎ 617/723-2500

🕐 Jul 5–Labor Day Sat–Thu 9–7, Fri 9–9. Labor Day–Jul 4 Sat–Thu 9–5, Fri 9–9. Extended hours over school holidays

🍴 Six on premises

Ⓢ Science Park

♿ Excellent. Sight- and hearing-impaired facilities

💲 Expensive. Separate tickets for Planetarium, Laser Show, Mugar Omni Theater. Combination ticket discounts. Boston CityPass applies

❓ Good shop

North End and Old North Church

- Paul Revere House (▷ 34)
- Old North Church Steeple
- Copp's Hill Burying Ground (▷ opposite)
- Feast-day processions
- Italian groceries, coffee shops and restaurants

- The North End explodes with life and color in late August for the Feast of St. Anthony.

The North End is Boston's oldest and most spirited district. This is where the British colonists settled in the 17th century, and now, after various ups and downs, it is a lively Italian quarter.

Little Italy The North End is separated from the rest of Boston by an area that was once a major highway, and is now a park. When the colonists arrived it was also all but cut off, surrounded then by water at the end of a narrow peninsula. The colonists' erratic street plan survives, but the only building from the 17th century is Paul Revere House. Once the elite had moved to Beacon Hill in the early 19th century, the area played host to waves of immigrants, first the Irish, then East Europeans and Portuguese and finally Italians who have given the area its current flavor.

The equestrian statue of Paul Revere with St. Stephen's Church beyond (left); Old North Church is now overshadowed by office buildings (middle); the decorative sign that welcomes visitors to North End (right)

WELCOME

BOSTON'S HISTORIC NORTH END

NORTH END BUSINESS ALLIANCE

Paul Revere Mall On Hanover Street, opposite St. Stephen's Church, the mall connects the North End's main street to Old North Church. This tree-shaded park is James Rego Square, but locals call it the Prado. Standing at one end is a bronze equestrian statue of Paul Revere (▷ panel, 125).

Old North Church It was from Old North that Revere's signal was given to the patriots in Charlestown that the British were on their way to Lexington where, the next day, the first battle of the War of Independence took place.

Copp's Hill Burying Ground Up the hill in front of Old North Church is a former Native American lookout point. In 1659 it became a burying ground, visited now for its rows of slate and stone headstones, many carved with winged skulls.

THE BASICS

www.oldnorth.com

✚ K4/K3

✉ Bounded by Commercial Street and Greenway

🕐 Old North Church: daily. Behind-the-scenes tours: Apr–Dec daily

🍴 Plenty around Hanover and Salem streets

🚇 Haymarket, North Station, Aquarium, State

♿ Some hills and uneven sidewalks

Old State House

HIGHLIGHTS

● Lion and unicorn
● Balcony from which the Declaration of Independence was read
● Exhibit showing topographical changes

TIPS

● Check the website for the latest events program.
● Don't miss the tiny phial of tea leaves saved from the Boston Tea Party.
● Light up the topographical map to see how much of Boston is built on landfill.

This is the city's oldest public building, once the seat of British colonial government. Surrounded by taller—but far less significant—buildings, it seems so tiny now. It holds a first-rate museum.

Colonial capital Built in 1713 to replace an earlier Town House, the Old State House was the British governor's seat of office, home to the judicial court and to the Massachusetts Assembly. The scene of many a confrontation between the colonists and their rulers, it was here that James Otis railed against the "tyranny of taxation without representation" and it was under the balcony at the east end that the "Boston Massacre" took place in 1770: Five colonists were killed in a clash with British soldiers, a key event in the years leading up

The Puritan interior of the Old State House (left) and the lion and unicorn on the east front (right)

to the Revolution. From the same balcony, the Declaration of Independence was read on July 18, 1776, and is still read every July 4. At this point the gilded lion and unicorn on the east front, symbols of the British Crown, were destroyed. From 1780 until 1798, this was the Massachusetts State House. It was used for commercial purposes, gradually falling into disrepair until the Bostonian Society was founded in 1881 to restore it. The lion and the unicorn were returned to their place, balanced now by the American eagle and the Massachusetts seal.

A Museum of Boston The building is home to the Bostonian Society's excellent museum, which traces the city's topographical, political, economic and social history, with a fine collection of maritime art and revolutionary memorabilia.

THE BASICS

www.bostonhistory.org
➕ K5
✉ 206 Washington Street
☎ 617/720-1713
🕐 Jun–Aug daily 9–6; Sep–May 9–5
🍴 Nearby
🚇 State, Government Center, Downtown Crossing
♿ No access to upper floor
💲 Inexpensive. Boston CityPass applies
❓ Shop

Paul Revere House

The bedroom (left) in Paul Revere House and views of the exterior (middle and right)

THE BASICS

www.paulreverehouse.org

🔲 K4

✉ 19 North Square

☎ 617/523-2338

🕐 Nov to mid-Apr daily 9.30–4.15; mid-Apr to Oct daily 9.30–5.15. Jan–Mar closed Mon

🍴 Nearby

Ⓜ Government Center, State, Aquarium, Haymarket

♿ Wheelchair access first floor only

✋ Inexpensive

❓ Tours of early Georgian Pierce/Hichborn House

HIGHLIGHTS

● Revere's own account of his ride
● Period furnishings

TIPS

● Avoid the house on spring and fall afternoons, when it is often overrun by groups of schoolchildren.
● Check ahead for the appearances by costumed interpreters.

This house is all that remains of the 17th-century settlement in today's North End. Not only is it Boston's oldest building, it was home to its most celebrated revolutionary, Paul Revere.

The early years The steep-gabled clapboard house that we see today was built in about 1680. Like most houses of the period, it had two rooms on both of its two floors but the positioning of the main staircase at the side of the building, making the rooms larger than normal, was unusual. By 1770, when the silversmith and engraver Paul Revere came to live here, significant alterations had been made, notably the addition of a third floor and a two-story extension at the back. The family lived here during the Revolution, so it was from here that Revere set out on that famous midnight ride (▷ panel, 125). In 1800, after the family sold the house, it became a rooming house, with stores and factory premises on the lower floor. Threatened with demolition in 1902, it was saved by Revere's great-grandson, restored to something like its origins and became a museum.

The house today The basic timber skeleton of the house is the original, but the exterior clap-boarding, the windows and most of what you see inside are replacements. Go through the kitchen into the living room, furnished in period style. Upstairs, the main bedroom is an elegantly furnished room, which would have doubled as a parlor. In the other room, note the ingenious folding bed and its traditional woven cover.

State House

State House (left) with its gleaming gold-leaf dome (right)

Prosperous and newly independent in the late 18th century, Massachusetts needed a larger, more imposing State House. Charles Bulfinch's masterpiece is a landmark in American architecture.

Hub of the Hub Bulfinch began designing the new State House on his return from England, much influenced by Robert Adam's Renaissance style. Construction began in 1795 on a prominent piece of Beacon Hill land. Cut off in your mind's eye the side wings (an early 20th-century addition), and focus on Bulfinch's dignified two-story portico and the glistening dome. Its original shingles were covered in copper from the foundry of Paul Revere when the roof began to leak, and the gold leaf was added in 1874. Until skyscrapers arrived, it dominated the city skyline.

Seat of government Start your tour in the columned Doric Hall. From here pass through the marble Nurses' Hall and note Bela Pratt's memorial to Civil War nurses. The Italian marble floor in the Hall of Flags was laid by immigrants from Italy. Featured in the stained-glass skylight are the seals of the original 13 states. Up the staircase is the House of Representatives chamber. Here, the Sacred Cod, a symbol of the importance of the fishing industry and a lucky mascot, must hang whenever the 160 state representatives are in session. The dignified barrel-vaulted and Ionic-columned Senate Reception Room is Bulfinch's, as is the Senate Chamber, where 40 senators debate beneath a graceful sunburst dome.

THE BASICS

www.sec.state.ma.us

🔲 J5

✉ Beacon Street

☎ 617/727-3676

🕐 Mon–Fri 10–3.30 (except holiday Mondays)

🍴 None

Ⓟ Park Street

♿ Partial wheelchair access

🆓 Free

❓ Regular tours (45 min); last tour 3.30. It is advisable to call in advance to reserve a guided tour

HIGHLIGHTS

● Gold dome (regilded in 1997 with 22 carat gold leaf)
● Sacred Cod
● Senate Reception Room
● Senate Chamber
● JFK statue

TIP

● To enter the State House for tours use the side entrance on Bowdoin Street.

USS *Constitution* and Charlestown

HIGHLIGHTS

● Museum: details of a sailor's daily diet and duties
● USS *Constitution*: cramped lower deck

TIPS

● If you are walking the Freedom Trail from Boston, get here by 3pm to take a tour of the ship.
● Kids will love the top floor of the museum, where they can fire ships' cannons in interactive games.

"Old Ironsides," as she is widely known by schoolchildren, is the oldest commissioned warship afloat in the world. More than 200 years old, she is moored in the Charlestown Navy Yard.

The Navy Yard From 1800 to 1974 the Charlestown Navy Yard played an important role building, repairing and supplying Navy warships. Its mission now is to interpret the history of naval shipbuilding. Representing the ships built here are USS *Constitution* and the World War II destroyer USS *Cassin Young*, both of which may be boarded. The old granite Building 22 now houses the USS *Constitution* Museum, where journals and objects record the frigate's 200-year career and give a picture of life aboard. Also open is the Commandant's House. The Bunker

Clockwise from far left: Gleaming cannons on the restored frigate USS Constitution, "Old Ironsides"; the world's oldest commissioned floating battleship, at dock in Charlestown Navy Yard; detail of the craftsmanship and rigging that have kept this venerable vessel afloat; view of the prow and masts; rigging winch

Hill Pavilion's diorama, "The Battle of Bunker Hill," tells the story of this battle. The Bunker Hill Monument stands atop the hill. It is visible from, and is within walking distance of, the Navy Yard. Climb its 294 steps for good views.

USS Constitution The highlight of the Yard is "Old Ironsides." Launched in Boston in 1797, she is still part of the US Navy, whose sailors lead tours round the cramped quarters. Vulnerable though the wooden sides seem now, it was her tough live-oak frames that enabled her to survive the War of 1812 undefeated and win her nickname. After surviving three wars, the vessel was frail and needed to be heavily reconstructed. She takes a turn in Boston Harbor every July 4, so that the side that faces the elements can be changed.

THE BASICS

www.history.navy.mil/
ussconstitution

www.nps.gov/bost

✚ K2/J2

✉ Charlestown Navy Yard

☎ Navy Yard Visitor
Center: 617/242-5601

🕐 USS *Constitution*
Museum: Apr–Oct 9–6;
Nov–Mar 10–5. USS
Constitution: Apr–Sep
Tue–Sun 10–6; Oct
Tue–Sun 10–4; Nov–Mar
Thu–Sat 10–4. USS *Cassin
Young*: Jul, Aug 10–5, Apr–
Jun, Sep–Nov 10–4. Closed
Dec–Mar. Bunker Hill
Monument: daily 9–4.30
(till 5.30 Jul–Aug). Bunker
Hill Museum: daily 9–5 (till
6 Jul–Aug)

🍴 In the Navy Yard

Ⓔ North Station or
Community College, then
15-min walk

🚢 MBTA Water Shuttle
from Long Wharf

♿ All wheelchair
accessible except
USS *Cassin Young*

⚡ All free except USS
Constitution Museum
(donation). 18s and over
need photo ID

More to See

AMES AND SEARS BUILDINGS
www.ameshotel.com
The 14-floor, 1889 Ames Building is now an elegant boutique hotel, the Ames (▷ 110).
🚇 K5 ✉ 1 Court Street 🚇 State

CHARLES RIVER BOAT TOURS
www.charlesriverboat.com
A leisurely cruise among the sailboats and crew teams on the Charles River offers a new perspective on the city, with views of Beacon Hill, the Boston skyline, the Esplanade and the Harvard residential houses. The Boston Harbor Sunset cruise is popular.
🚇 H3 ✉ 100 CambridgeSide Place, Suite 320, Cambridge ☎ 617/621-3001 🕐 Hours vary by season; call for details 🚇 Lechmere 💲 Expensive ❓ Main docking location at Canal Park, CambridgeSide Galleria, Cambridge

CHRISTOPHER COLUMBUS WATERFRONT PARK
This is a small waterfront park near Faneuil Hall Marketplace and North End. Sit under the trellis or on the grass with a picnic and watch the boats.
🚇 L4 ✉ Atlantic Avenue 🚇 Aquarium 🕐 Daily 💲 Free

CUSTOM HOUSE TOWER
The 30-floor clock tower, built in 1915, is a Boston landmark and was for a long time the city's tallest building. At street level you see how odd it looks stuck on the roof of the original Custom House, built in 1847 in Greek Revival style, at what was then the water's edge. It is now a hotel, but the public can go up to the observatory for great views.
🚇 K5 ✉ 3 McKinley Square 🕐 Observatory: Sat–Thu at 2pm 🚇 State, Aquarium 💲 Donation to charity

JAMES CURLEY STATUES
A colorful Boston Irish mayor, James Curley (1874–1958) comes both seated and standing (Lloyd Lillie, 1980) at Faneuil Hall.
🚇 K4 ✉ North/Union streets 🚇 State

The Custom House Tower at night

Commercial Wharf adjacent to Christopher Columbus Park on the waterfront

MUSEUM OF AFRICAN AMERICAN HISTORY

www.afroammuseum.org

A museum dedicated to the history of African-Americans in Boston is housed in the 1806 African Meeting House. Once a center for social and political activity, it is now a focal point on the Black Heritage Trail, a 1.6-mile (2.5km) guided or self-guided walking tour of pre-Civil War Beacon Hill sites, including the Abiel Smith School and the Robert Gould Shaw Monument.

➕ J5 ✉ 46 Joy Street ☎ 617/725-0022 🕐 Mon–Sat 10–4 🚇 Charles/MGH, Park Street, Government Center 💷 Inexpensive

NEW ENGLAND HOLOCAUST MEMORIAL

www.nehm.org

Six tall glass towers, the work of Stanley Saitowitz (1995), recall Nazi death camps. Etched numerals represent the Holocaust's six million victims. The memorial is especially poignant after dark, when floodlit.

➕ K4 ✉ Union Street 🕐 Daily 🚇 State

NICHOLS HOUSE MUSEUM

www.nicholshousemuseum.org

One of Boston's earliest Federal-style houses, this elegant four-floor Beacon Hill house was built by Charles Bulfinch in 1804 and is furnished with Nichols family art and antiques.

➕ J5 ✉ 55 Mount Vernon Street ☎ 617/227-6993 🕐 Apr–Oct Tue–Sat 11–4; Nov–Mar Thu–Sat 11–4. By tour only; last tour starts at 4pm 🚇 Park Street 💷 Moderate

SAMUEL ADAMS STATUE

Anne Whitney's (1880) portrayal of the defiant revolutionary leader Samuel Adams stands in front of Faneuil Hall.

➕ K5 ✉ Congress Street 🚇 State

TD GARDEN

www.tdgarden.com

The old West End is not an exciting district, but the TD Garden sports stadium is the home of the Celtics (basketball) and Bruins (ice hockey).

➕ J3 ✉ 100 Legends Way 🎫 Ticketmaster: 800/745-3000 🚇 North Station

Statue of Paul Revere in front of the Old North Church

The African Meeting House hosts the Museum of African American History

reedom Trail

The Freedom Trail links sites from Boston's Colonial and revolutionary era. Follow the red line on the sidewalk (pictured above).

DISTANCE: 1.5 miles (2.5km) **ALLOW:** 1–4 hours

START

BOSTON COMMON (▷ 50)
✚ J5 🚇 Park Street

END

COPP'S HILL (▷ 31)
✚ K3 🚇 North Station

❶ From the information center on Boston Common head for the State House (▷ 35). Walk down Park Street to "Brimstone Corner" where gunpowder was stored.

❽ Back in Hanover Street, turn onto Revere Mall, passing Paul Revere's statue (▷ 30–31), with the Old North Church (▷ 31) steeple ahead. Continue uphill to Copp's Hill.

❷ On Tremont Street, in the Granary Burying Ground, find the graves of many famous people. King's Chapel (▷ 55) is the oldest church site in Boston still in use.

❼ Cross Blackstone Street and cross the Rose Kennedy Greenway to the North End. Turn onto Richmond Street to reach North Square and Paul Revere House (▷ 34).

❸ On School Street a sidewalk mosaic marks the site of the first free school, open to all. Pass the statue of Benjamin Franklin.

❻ The trail continues between the New England Holocaust Memorial (▷ 39) and the Union Oyster House (▷ 46) to Hanover Street.

❹ Diagonally right, past the Irish Famine Memorial (▷ 55), is Old South Meeting House (▷ 56), where the Boston Tea Party started. Follow the red line along Washington Street to Old State House (▷ 32–33).

❺ Cross onto Congress Street to get to Faneuil Hall (▷ 26).

Shopping

BEACON HILL CHOCOLATES

www.beaconhillchocolates.com
Fine chocolate is transformed into delectable and beautiful gifts, packaged in elegant boxes. The tiny shop's entrance is just around the corner from Charles Street.
🔲 H5 ✉ 91 Charles Street ☎ 617/725-1900 Ⓣ Charles/MGH

BLACK INK

blackinkboston.squarespace.com
An eclectic selection of funky gifts and novelties: shark staplers, alphabet cookie cutters, bright green frog banks, architectural city guides.
🔲 H5 ✉ 101 Charles Street ☎ 617/723-3883 Ⓣ Charles/MGH, Arlington

BOSTON PEWTER COMPANY

bostonpewtercompany.com
All manner of traditional, hand-crafted pewter items fill shelves here, including pieces for the home (lighting, sculpture and dishes) and giftware (picture frames, jewelry).
🔲 K5 ✉ South Market, Faneuil Hall Marketplace ☎ 617/523-1776 Ⓣ State, Government Center

BOSTONIAN SOCIETY MUSEUM SHOP

www.bostonhistory.org
Buy a little piece of New England history from this store, created to support Boston's Historical Society. The group peddles books about New England's past, plus quilts, teas, mugs and prints.
🔲 K5 ✉ South Canopy, Faneuil Hall Marketplace ☎ 617/742-4744 Ⓣ State, Government Center

BUILD-A-BEAR WORKSHOP

www.buildabear.com
Teddy bears are the focus, although this shop has plush dinosaurs and other stuffed animals too. Everything the well-dressed bear needs is here: clothes, boots, paw brushes, Santa beards, furniture, sandals and all the latest in bearwear.
🔲 K5 ✉ North Market, Faneuil Hall Marketplace ☎ 617/227-2478 Ⓣ Government Center/State

CAMBRIDGESIDE GALLERIA

www.cambridgesidegalleria.com
More than 120 stores and restaurants includ-

THE CHAIN

Most of the major American clothes chains are represented in the city: Abercrombie & Fitch (Faneuil Hall Marketplace), Banana Republic (CambridgeSide Galleria, Newbury Street), Giorgio Armani (Newbury Street), Saks Fifth Avenue, Ann Taylor, Lacoste, Lord & Taylor, Gucci, Vera Bradley, Samsonite and Chico's (Prudential Center).

---

ing Gap, Sears, Macy's, Best Buy, California Pizza Kitchen and the Cheesecake Factory.
🔲 G3 ✉ 100 CambridgeSide Place ☎ 617/621-8666 Ⓣ Lechmere

COACH

www.coach.com
This popular and high-quality international leather goods company sells an impressive selection of the collection's handbags, business gear, shoes and other accessories. Also at Copley Place.
🔲 K5 ✉ South Market, Faneuil Hall Marketplace ☎ 617/723-1777 Ⓣ State, Government Center

DANISH COUNTRY ANTIQUES

www.europeanstyleantiques.com
True to its name, this gem full of imported finds sells well-preserved, rustic pieces from Denmark. Don't miss the fine selection of tables—for the kitchen, dining room or living room.
🔲 H4 ✉ 138 Charles Street ☎ 617/227-1804 Ⓣ Charles/MGH

EUGENE GALLERIES

eugenegalleries.com
Specializes in old maps and prints, with a good selection covering Boston. This is the place to discover heirlooms and excellent gifts.
🔲 H5 ✉ 76 Charles Street ☎ 617/227-3062 Ⓣ Charles/MGH

FLAT OF THE HILL
www.flatofthehill.com
Charming gift boutique crammed with garden accessories, hand-knit throws, pretty stationery and more.
✚ H5 ✉ 60 Charles Street
☎ 617/619-9977 🚇 Charles/MGH

GEOCLASSICS
www.geoclassics.com
Geological wonders become fine jewelry, displayed to show their origin.
✚ K5 ✉ 7 North Market, Faneuil Hall Marketplace
☎ 617/523-6112
🚇 Government Center, State

GOOD, INC
www.shopatgood.com
A range of simple but design-conscious gifts.
✚ H4 ✉ 133 Charles Street
☎ 617/722-9200 🚇 Charles/MGH

HILTON'S TENT CITY
hiltontentcity.com
Good place for hiking and camping equipment and performance clothing.
✚ K4 ✉ 272 Friend Street
☎ 617/227-9242 🚇 North Station

HOLIDAY BOUTIQUE
www.holidayboutique.net
Modern, sassy women's fashions line the racks of this small but well-stocked shop. As well as in-house Holiday creations, find one-of-a-kind designs by Eva Franco, Ecru, David Lerner, J Brand and Kirribilla.

✚ H5 ✉ 53 Charles Street
☎ 617/973-9730 🚇 Charles/MGH

LINENS ON THE HILL
www.linensonthehill.com
Fine French linens: sheets, pillowcases, tablecloths, nightgowns, robes.
✚ H6 ✉ 52 Charles Street
☎ 617/227-1255 🚇 Charles/MGH, Arlington

noa
www.noagifts.com
This store specializes in unusual jewelry, fine handcrafts and gifts made by some 25 New England artisans.
✚ H5 ✉ 88 Charles Street
☎ 857/233-4912 🚇 Charles/MGH

OFFICINA 189
www.officina189.com
High-quality scarves, handbags and perfumes, bicycles and watches, leather and jewelry from small, high-class designers. This concept store bills itself as a MUSHOP, part museum, part shop.
✚ K4 ✉ 189 North Street,

CHARLES STREET
This is a delightful street of stores and restaurants, running north from the Public Garden through the flat area of Beacon Hill. It specializes in (mostly pricey) antiques shops but has several gift shops and galleries, too, and a selection of places where you can get a bite to eat.
✚ J4 🚇 Arlington, Charles

North End ☎ 857/233-4300
🚇 Haymarket

PERIOD FURNITURE HARDWARE CO.
www.periodfurniturehardware.com
For those awkward-to-find details that owners of older houses need: doorknobs, window latches, coat hooks and weathervanes. Plus lighting, faucets and fireplaces.
✚ H5 ✉ 123 Charles Street
☎ 617/227-0758 🚇 Charles/MGH

THE RED WAGON
www.theredwagon.com
Bright, creatively casual T-shirt sets, dresses and more for babies and young children.
✚ H5 ✉ 69 Charles Street
☎ 617/524-9402 🚇 Charles/MGH

SAVENOR'S
www.savenorsmarket.com
The late, mighty culinary queen Julia Child used to order her meats from this specialty foods market, where you'll find everything from giraffe meat to wild mushrooms.
✚ H5 ✉ 160 Charles Street ☎ 617/723-6328
🚇 Charles/MGH

WISH BOUTIQUE
wishboston.com
Colorful women's clothing store, with frocks by Nanette Lapore, Rebecca Taylor and Theory.
✚ H5 ✉ 49 Charles Street ☎ 617/227-4441
🚇 Charles/MGH

Entertainment and Nightlife

21ST AMENDMENT

www.21stboston.com
Across from the State House, a good spot to refuel with beer and specialty sandwiches while walking the Freedom Trail. At night, it attracts a young local crowd.
➕ J5 ✉ 150 Bowdoin Street ☎ 617/227-7100 🚇 Bowdoin, Park Street

BEACON HILL PUB

A good old-fashioned neighborhood pub favored by students as well as locals for its inexpensive drinks, a dozen beers on tap, darts and a jukebox. It serves no food and boasts no frills.
➕ H5 ✉ 149 Charles Street ☎ 617/625-7100 🚇 Charles/MGH

THE BLACK ROSE

www.blackroseboston.com
This family Irish bar is one of the best places to catch live Celtic music—and to line your stomach with corned beef and Guinness.
➕ J5 ✉ 160 State Street ☎ 617/742-2286 🚇 State

CHEERS

www.cheersboston.org
After standing in line for hours, tourists are often disappointed that the inside of the Bull & Finch on Beacon Hill, which served as the model for the television show Cheers, looks nothing like it does on TV. Instead, go by the new Cheers bar in

Faneuil Hall, which was designed to be an exact replica of the set.
➕ K5 ✉ 84 Beacon Street / Faneuil Hall Marketplace ☎ 617/227-9605 or 617/227-0150 🚇 Charles/MGH, Arlington, Haymarket

HONG KONG AT FANEUIL HALL

www.hongkongboston.com
Two words: scorpion bowls! The booze-filled punch packs a wallop, and fuels a fun but cheesy dance scene.
➕ K5 ✉ 65 Chatham Street ☎ 617/227-2226 🚇 State

IMPROV ASYLUM

www.improvasylum.com
Comedy theater that features sketch and improvisational comedy at a North End cabaret-style

NIGHTLIFE AND CRUISES
Odyssey
Operates evening cruises on a 600-passenger yacht, plus a Sunday jazz brunch and weekday lunches (reservations required).
✉ Rowes Wharf ☎ 617/654-9710 or 866/307-2469; www.odysseycruises.com
The Spirit of Boston
Has DJs and shows on its dinner-dance cruises.
✉ World Trade Center ☎ 617/748-1450; www.spiritcruises.com
🕐 Lunch and dinner cruises daily Jun–Oct. Call for winter schedule

theater. Advance tickets recommended.
➕ K4 ✉ 216 Hanover Street ☎ 617/263-6887 🕐 Shows Tue–Sun 🚇 Haymarket

LAST HURRAH

www.omnihotels.com
Black-and-white photos from Boston's Golden Age line the walls in the Parker House's upscale hotel bar. Clientele is a mix of hotel guests and City Hall politicos.
➕ K5 ✉ 60 School Street ☎ 617/227-8600 🚇 Government Center, State

SEVENS

Often referred to as the "real Cheers," this Charles Street institution draws a slice from all walks of life to drink frosty ones at wooden booths and gripe about the Sox.
➕ H5 ✉ 77 Charles Street ☎ 617/523-9074 🚇 Charles/MGH

WARREN TAVERN

www.warrentavern.com
Open since 1780, this is arguably America's most historic watering hole. The pub is named for Doctor Warren, the patriot who ordered Paul Revere and William Dawes to ride to Lexington on the evening of April 18, 1775. It boasts an A List of visitors, including George Washington and Paul Revere. Hearty pub food, interesting beers.
➕ J2 ✉ 2 Pleasant Street, Charlestown ☎ 617/241-8142 🚇 Community College

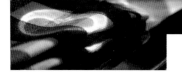

Restaurants

PRICES

Prices are approximate, based on a 3-course meal for one person.
$$$ over $40
$$ $20–$40
$ under $20

ANTHEM KITCHEN + BAR ($$)

www.anthem-boston.com
Modern takes on heart-warming comfort food, from crab cakes, lobster rolls and chicken with mashed potatoes to meatloaf, burgers, even lobster mac and cheese.
⊞ K5 ✉ South Market Building, Faneuil Hall ☎ 617/720-5570 🕐 Lunch, dinner daily, Sunday breakfast 🚇 State, Government Center

ANTICO FORNO ($)

Excellent Italian specialties at this casual, small spot, all whisked from the brick oven to your table. Try the fusilli with vegetables, goat cheese and basil or the swordfish with citrus and pickled onions.
⊞ K4 ✉ 93 Salem Street ☎ 617/723-6733 🕐 Lunch, dinner daily 🚇 Haymarket

ARTÙ ($$)

Country-style Italian cooking and friendly staff. Try chicken layered with eggplant and mozzarella. There is a second branch at 89 Charles Street.
⊞ K4 ✉ 6 Prince Street, North End ☎ 617/742-4336 🕐 Lunch, dinner daily 🚇 Haymarket

BEACON HILL BISTRO ($$)

A soothing, neutral-toned bistro serving excellent seafood dishes and a creative late-night bar menu. Don't miss top-notch desserts like the rhubarb clafouti with macerated strawberries.
⊞ H5 ✉ 25 Charles Street ☎ 617/723-7575 🕐 Breakfast, lunch, dinner daily 🚇 Charles/MGH

CAFFÈ VITTORIA ($)

Popular North End spot for an after-dinner coffee, pastry or gelato.
⊞ K4 ✉ 296 Hanover Street ☎ 617/227-7606 🕐 Daily 7am–midnight 🚇 Haymarket

CANTINA ITALIANA ($$)

A relaxed eatery serving excellent regional food.
⊞ K4 ✉ 346 Hanover Street, North End ☎ 617/723-4577 🕐 Mon–Sat from 11.30; Sun from noon 🚇 Haymarket

SEAFOOD OPTIONS

Nowadays some of Boston's finest fish is not only served in the traditional seafood restaurants listed on these pages. Most of the city's best eating spots do an excellent job with seafood preparations, and these dishes are taking an increasingly large share of their menus. Other good choices for fresh seafood are any of the Chinatown restaurants with fresh-from-the-tanks fish.

DURGIN PARK ($$)

www.durgin-park.com
One of the oldest dining rooms in the US. The roast beef melts in the mouth and there's hard-to-find traditional fare like Indian pudding. Crowded; very informal—but the waiters make a thing of being rude.
⊞ K5 ✉ Faneuil Hall Marketplace ☎ 617/227-2038 🕐 Daily 11.30–10 🚇 State, Aquarium, Government Center

FALAFEL KING ($)

Quick service in a busy area offering well-priced chicken and lamb kebobs, as well as falafel.
⊞ K5 ✉ 260 Washington Street, Downtown Crossing ☎ 617/227-6400 🕐 Mon–Fri 11–6; Sat 11–3.30 🚇 Downtown Crossing, State

LA FAMIGLIA GIORGIO'S RESTAURANT ($$)

All the favorites, in generous portions, are served at this family-friendly Roman-style restaurant. Teachers and students with ID get 20 percent discount, and the children's menu offers more choices than most.
⊞ K4 ✉ 112 Salem Street ☎ 617/367-6711 🕐 Lunch and dinner daily 🚇 Haymarket

HUNGRY I ($$$)

Tiny, intimate basement offering a small but inventive menu.
⊞ H5 ✉ 71 Charles Street ☎ 617/227-3524 🕐 Lunch

Thu–Fri; dinner daily; brunch Sun 🚇 Charles/MGH

LALA ROKH ($$)
www.lalarokh.com
Refined Persian cuisine at this elegant restaurant. Specialties include exotic creations like chicken with rose petals, cumin and cinnamon. The saffron ice cream is a must-try.
🚹 H5 ✉ 97 Mount Vernon Street ☎ 617/720-5511 🕐 Lunch Mon–Fri, dinner daily 🚇 Charles/MGH

MAMMA MARIA ($$$)
www.mammamaria.com
Highly regarded elegant North End Italian, offering imaginative cooking and gracious service. Try the osso buco.
🚹 K4 ✉ 3 North Square, North End ☎ 617/523-0077 🕐 Dinner daily 🚇 Haymarket

MARIA'S PASTRY SHOP ($)
mariaspastry.com
From creating award-winning cannoli and chocolate torrone to tiramisu and Italian cheese cake, the Merola family ensure that Maria's is all about the sweet things in life.
🚹 K4 ✉ 46 Cross Street, North End ☎ 617/523-1196 🕐 Daily 7–7, Sun 7–5 🚇 Haymarket

NEPTUNE OYSTER ($$)
www.neptuneoyster.com
New Englanders are justly proud of their seafood, and this raw bar serves the freshest and best: Wellfleet clams, littlenecks and cherrystones. Carry on with chowders, whole roasted fish and lobster clambake.
🚹 K4 ✉ 63 Salem Street, North End ☎ 617/742-3474 🕐 Daily 11.30–9.30, weekends till 10.30 🚇 State, Government Center

NO. 9 PARK ($$$)
New American fare in a dignified if simple dining room. Chef Barbara Lynch has a way with duck; her signature crispy duck is deliciously crisp outside and meltingly tender within. Less expensive café menu.
🚹 J5 ✉ 9 Park Street ☎ 617/742-9991 🕐 Dinner nightly 🚇 Park Street

PARAMOUNT ($$)
www.paramountboston.com
After 75 years, this family restaurant still delivers good value and quality: chicken marsala, salmon burgers and BBQ sirloin steak tips.

NEW ENGLAND DISHES

Try these: lobster, clam chowder, scrod, quahog (a large clam, pronounced "ko hog"), Boston baked beans (slow-cooked for flavor in an earthenware pot), Boston cream pie (chocolate-covered and custard-filled white cake) and Indian pudding (cornmeal, milk and molasses, cooked long and slow).

🚹 H5 ✉ 44 Charles Street ☎ 617/720-1152 🕐 Daily 7am–10pm, 8am–11pm weekends 🚇 Charles/MGH

PREZZA ($$$)
www.prezza.com
Modern Italian fare in a hip space. Try the homemade pastas such as pea tortelli with Virginia ham. Save room for the chocolate hazelnut cake.
🚹 L4 ✉ 24 Fleet Street, North End ☎ 617/227-1577 🕐 Dinner daily 🚇 Haymarket

UNION OYSTER HOUSE ($$)
www.unionoysterhouse.com
More regarded as an historic landmark than an eatery, Union Oyster House has been open since 1826, and has hosted everyone from John F. Kennedy to Leonardo DiCaprio.
🚹 K4 ✉ 41 Union Street ☎ 617/227-2750 🕐 Lunch, dinner daily 🚇 Haymarket

UPPER CRUST PIZZERIA ($)
www.theuppercrustpizzeria.com
Uncommonly good, gourmet pizzas at the original Upper Crust location—all thin-crusted, and all straight out of the oven. The Margherita is a favorite, but don't bypass other toppings such as baby clams, prosciutto, *asiago* and pineapple.
🚹 H5 ✉ 20 Charles Street ☎ 617/723-9600 🕐 Lunch, dinner daily 🚇 Charles/MGH

Boston Common to the Waterfront

The bustling area running from Boston Common and the Public Garden to the Waterfront takes you through the Theater District, Chinatown and the Financial District.

Sights	50–56	Top 25	TOP 25
Walk	57	Boston Common and Public Garden ▷ 50	
Shopping	58	Boston Tea Party Ships and Museum ▷ 51	
Entertainment and Nightlife	59–60	Institute of Contemporary Art ▷ 52	
Restaurants	61–62	New England Aquarium ▷ 53	

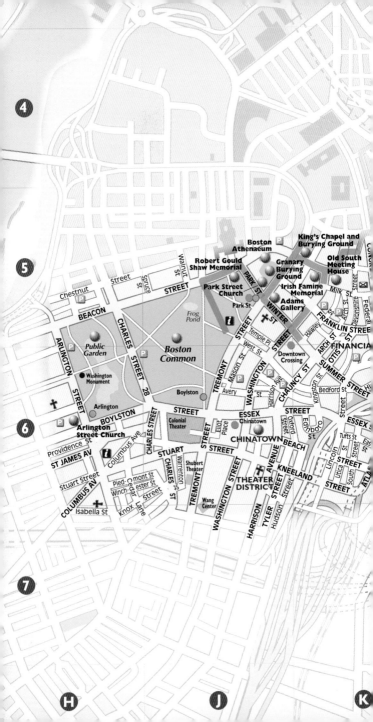

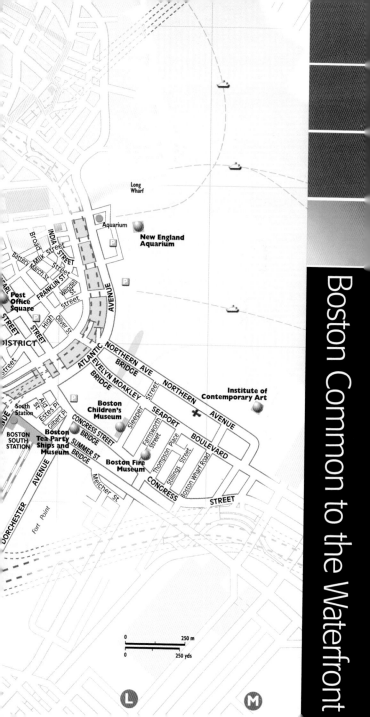

Long Wharf

Aquarium

New England Aquarium

INDIA STREET

Broad Street

Batter March St

Milk Street

FRANKLIN STREET

Wendell St

High Street

Oliver St

Post Office Square

AVENUE

DISTRICT

Street

ATLANTIC

NORTHERN AVE BRIDGE

EVELYN MOAKLEY BRIDGE

NORTHERN

AVENUE

Institute of Contemporary Art

South Station

Alg

Estes Pl

Gilbert Pl

CONGRESS STREET

Boston Children's Museum

Sleeper Street

SEAPORT

Farnsworth Street

Thompson Place

BOULEVARD

Boston Wharf Road

BOSTON SOUTH STATION

Boston Tea Party Ships and Museum

SUMMER ST BRIDGE

CONGRESS BRIDGE

Boston Fire Museum

Stillings Street

CONGRESS

STREET

AVENUE

DORCHESTER

Melcher St

Fort Point

0   250 m

0   250 yds

L   M

Boston Common and Public Garden

Pedal-powered Swan Boats, which date from 1877, transport visitors around the lagoon

THE BASICS

✚ J5/H5

✉ Bounded by Beacon, Park, Tremont, Boylston, Arlington streets

☎ Swan Boats: 617/ 522-1966. Ice-skating: 617/635-2120

🕐 Public Garden: daily dawn–10pm. Swan Boats: Apr–Sep. Ice-skating: Dec–Mar

🍴 Nearby

Ⓣ Park Street, Boylston, Arlington

♿ Garden and Common free. Swan Boats, skating inexpensive

TIPS

● The Common's Parkman Bandstand frequently features free concerts and plays.

● Try to avoid bringing a car into Central Boston, but if you must, beneath Boston Common is one of the most affordable garages (enter from Charles Street).

Very different in history and character, these adjoining pieces of public open space, separated by Charles Street, right in the heart of the city, are held in deep affection. Without them, Boston just wouldn't be Boston.

Boston Common The oldest public park in the US owes its origins to early British settlers who in 1634 acquired the land from a Reverend William Blaxton for common grazing. It was also where criminals were hanged, witches were dunked and the dead were buried (in the Central Burying Ground, by Boylston Street). Here, British soldiers camped and George Washington addressed the crowds after Independence. Early in the 1800s paths were laid out and fountains and monuments erected. It is still a place for speeches and demonstrations, but also for street performers and concerts or, in winter, ice-skating at Frog Pond. Safe by day, it's best avoided at night.

The Public Garden This was created as a botanical garden in 1837. Hundreds of trees were planted and beds, lawns and footpaths were laid out. The garden is perennially beautiful and often fairy-tale-like. The focal point is a lagoon, with a little cast-iron suspension bridge (once the world's smallest). Here, in summer, you can ride the famous Swan Boats. Sculptures include a striking equestrian George Washington (Thomas Ball, 1869) and the Ether Monument, marking the first use of ether as an anaesthetic, here in Boston, in 1846.

Visitors dump parcels of tea over the side of the Boston Tea Party Ship

Boston Tea Party Ships and Museum

Every American child learns about the night of December 16, 1773, when tea was dumped in Boston Harbor. But aboard the *Eleanor* and the *Beaver*, the drama comes to life with actors and visitor participation.

Spirit of '73 Much of what occurred when the Sons of Liberty boarded three ships in Boston Harbor and threw cargo overboard is still blurred by patriotic fervor. Here, visitors from the USA and abroad can reconsider the facts and argue out the complex whys and wherefores. They do so by playing authentic historic roles, reading out scripts handed out to them by staff dressed in period costume. The action-packed one-hour tour gets under way in the replica meeting house, where Sam Adams makes a fiery speech. The arguments for and against revolt are rehearsed. On the two replica ships, moored alongside, everyone gets to "dump the tea" overboard.

Meet the king Among the authentic artifacts in the museum is a 230-year-old "half-chest," one of only two existing tea chests that were thrown in the harbor. Grabbing the attention are holograms, oil paintings of King George III, John Hancock and Lord North that spring into life and carry out a "debate" about the right to impose taxes. An award-winning movie leads visitors on to the clashes in April, 1775, in Concord and Lexington, just west of Boston. This provides a thought-provoking introduction to the events that led up to the American Revolution.

THE BASICS

www.bostonteapartyship.com

🚇 L6

✉ Congress Street Bridge

☎ 617/338-1773

🕐 Daily 10–4; tours begin every 30 mins

🍴 Abigail's Tea Room

🚇 South Station

♿ Wheelchair access to museum and ship

💲 Expensive; online discount

❓ Annual Boston Tea Party Reenactment, Dec 16

HIGHLIGHTS

● Visitors get involved with the politics
● Meeting the 18th-century characters
● The holograms
● Views of the harbor

TIP

● A great family day out, combined with nearby Boston Children's Museum.

Institute of Contemporary Art

TOP 25

The superb home of the Institute (left); The Founders' Gallery (right)

The catalyst for South Boston's revitalized waterfront district is the ICA, set in a dramatic building that hangs out over the water. The building, with its contemporary art, is right on the HarborWalk that reconnects the city with its roots.

The building The first US work of the architectural firm of Diller Scofidio + Renfro, the dramatic building reaches out over the harbor with a breathtaking cantilevered facade. Its expanses of glass overlook superb views, and the area sheltered by the overhang creates an amphitheater for performances with the water as a backdrop.

The art Superb though the views may be, the building also offers extraordinary opportunities for displaying contemporary art and mounting multimedia presentations. The Institute's permanent collection of 21st-century art includes works by leading names, among them Philip-Lorca diCorcia, Mona Hatoum, Ambreen Butt, Paul Chan, Rineke Dijkstra and Thomas Hirschorn. As the museum's holdings continue to grow, the main emphasis is on the well-interpreted special exhibitions that explore the complex nature of artistic expression.

HarborWalk Part of a planned 47-mile (76km) promenade that will cover Boston's entire waterfront, the section of HarborWalk that connects Rowe's Wharf to the Institute is worth walking for its own art. In addition to the harbor views, the walkway is lined with beautiful iron sculptures representing marine themes.

THE BASICS

www.icaboston.org
- M6
- 100 Northern Avenue
- 617/478-3100, Box Office 617/478-3103
- Tue–Wed, Sat–Sun 10–5, Thu–Fri 10–9
- Water Café on site
- Courthouse
- Wheelchair access
- Expensive (free Thu 5–9pm and for families the last Sat of each month, excluding Dec)
- Performances, concerts

HIGHLIGHTS

- The architecture
- The interpretation of exhibits
- The outstanding gift shop

TIP

- While in the neighborhood, enjoy lunch or dinner at Aura (▷ 61), a few steps down Northern Avenue in the Seaport Hotel.

New England Aquarium

A replica coral reef home to tropical fish (left); the modern aquarium building (right)

One of the largest aquatic collections in the world, this is a popular family excursion. A spiral ramp leads you around a vast cylindrical tank swirling with sea creatures of every imaginable size, shape and hue.

Penguins, sharks and electric eels In the penguin pool at the base of the Giant Ocean Tank pick out the world's smallest penguin species, the Little Blues, then head left, past the Medical Center. Either go outside for a sea-lion presentation or turn right, up the straight ramp, to the Thinking Gallery, where you can compare your hearing to that of a dolphin and your skeleton to that of a fish. The Freshwater Gallery has above- and below-surface views of a flooded Amazon forest complete with anaconda, alongside, by contrast, a New England trout stream. Don't miss the electric eel. Eventually, you reach the top of the huge tank at the heart of the Aquarium. At feeding times, approximately hourly, staff dive in, scattering squid for the bigger fish, jamming lettuce into the fiberglass coral reef for the angel fish, hand-feeding the sharks and giving the turtles their vitamin-enriched gelatin (to keep their shells hard). Notice how all the fish swim in the same direction, into the current set up by the filter, to get more oxygen.

From big screen to deep waters To experience places that cannot be re-created in the aquarium, watch one of the aquatic films showing at the IMAX theater. Alternatively, take the excellent Voyager III whale-watching trip.

THE BASICS

www.neaq.org

➕ L5

✉ Central Wharf

☎ 617/973-5200

🕐 Jul 1–Labor Day Sun–Thu 9–6, Fri–Sat, holidays 9–7; rest of year Mon–Fri 9–5, Sat, Sun, holidays 9–6

🍴 On premises

Ⓜ Aquarium 🛗 Good

💲 Expensive (IMAX is extra). Boston CityPass applies

❓ Concerts, lectures, tours, shop, whale-watching Apr–Oct ☎ 617/973-5200

HIGHLIGHTS

● Giant Ocean Tank
● Medical Center
● The huge green sea turtle
● Little blue penguins
● Whale-watching trip
● IMAX 3D films

TIPS

● Book two weeks in advance for a special "behind the scenes" family tour ($14 per person).
● Check the daily schedule for training sessions, feeding times and shows.

More to See

ADAMS GALLERY

www.suffolk.edu/adamsgallery
The history and culture of Boston and New England provides plenty of themes for collections and exhibits in this storefront gallery opposite Park Street Church (▷ 56). Everything from the Red Sox to home milk delivery have been featured in this interesting stop along the Freedom Trail.
✚ J5 ✉ Suffolk University Law School, 120 Tremont Street ☎ 617/305-1782
🕐 Daily 9–7 🚇 Park Street

ARLINGTON STREET CHURCH

www.ascboston.org
If the church is closed, ask the staff in the office (at the back) to open up. It has the largest collection of Tiffany windows in any one church.
✚ H6 ✉ Boylston Street at Arlington Street. Office: 351 Boylston Street 🕐 Office: Mon–Fri 9–5 🚇 Arlington

BOSTON ATHENAEUM

www.bostonathenaeum.org
The name may look odd today, but this was the cultural and intellectual heart of the city when it opened in 1807. Members used the library, admired the art collection, met friends and argued beneath the lavishly decorated interiors. Today, anyone can visit the first floor and exhibition galleries, but to appreciate the rare books and works of art, take a free, hour-long, docent-led Art and Architecture Tour (Tue, Thu at 3).
✚ J5 ✉ 101/2 Beacon Street ☎ 617/227-0270, ext. 279 🕐 Mon–Wed 9–8, Thu–Fri 9–5.30, Sat 9–4 🚇 Park

BOSTON CHILDREN'S MUSEUM

www.bostonchildrensmuseum.org
When it opened in 1913, this was only the second children's museum in the world. It's heaven on earth for under-10s. Try the balance climb, play at shops with life-size products, squirt water jets at model boats, stretch a gigantic bubble or just enjoy the play space. And when you're all exhausted, retreat to the peace and quiet of the Japanese house.
✚ L6 ✉ 308 Congress Street, Museum Wharf ☎ 617/426-6500 🕐 Daily 10–5

Colorful neon lights inside the Children's Museum

(Fri until 9) 🍴 Several nearby 🚇 South Station 💷 Moderate (Fri 5–9 $1)

BOSTON FIRE MUSEUM
www.bostonfiremuseum.com
Housed in the old firehouse on Congress Street, the museum displays shiny antique fire engines dating back to 1793, a variety of fire alarms and fire-fighting memorabilia from Boston's fires, including the great fire of 1872 and the 1942 Cocoanut Grove disaster.
➕ L6 ✉ 344 Congress Street
☎ 617/338-9700 🕐 Sat 11–4 🚇 South Station 💷 Donation

CHINATOWN
www.chinatownmainstreet.org
Although small, the blocks between Essex Street and Kneeland Street are intensely Asian. The third largest Chinese community in the United States keeps the grocery stores, markets and bakeries thriving, and visitors join them to keep its many restaurants humming.
➕ J6 🚇 Chinatown, South Station

IRISH FAMINE MEMORIAL
These 1998 bronzes commemorate those forced by the 1840s Potato Famine to leave their native Ireland.
➕ K5 ✉ Washington/School streets

GRANARY BURYING GROUND
If you see only one burial ground, make it this one. Dating from 1660, it's the leafy resting place of many of Boston's big names—Samuel Adams, Paul Revere, James Otis, John Hancock and Peter Faneuil. Throughout, informative sign boards add historic information about the carved headstones, the people buried here and events that shaped early Boston. Many of these help to bring the place and the Colonial era to life.
➕ J5 ✉ 88 Tremont Street 🚇 Park Street

KING'S CHAPEL AND BURYING GROUND
www.kings-chapel.org
This was built as an Anglican church in 1687 on the orders of King James II, to the indignation of the Puritan

King's Chapel later became the city's first Unitarian Church

colonists. In the town's earliest (1630) burial ground lie two *Mayflower* passengers and John Winthrop, first governor of Massachusetts.

✚ K5 ✉ Tremont/School streets ☎ 617/227-2155 🕐 Hours vary–call ahead. No tourists during services 🚇 Park Street

OLD SOUTH MEETING HOUSE

www.oldsouthmeetinghouse.org

Starting life in 1729 as a Puritan meeting house, this was the site of the meeting that started the Boston Tea Party in 1773.

✚ K5 ✉ 310 Washington Street ☎ 617/482-6439 🕐 Apr–Oct daily 9.30–5; Nov–Mar daily 10–4 🚇 State, Downtown Crossing 💷 Moderate

PARK STREET CHURCH

www.parkstreet.org

Notable as much for its tall, white steeple as for William Lloyd Garrison's first anti-slavery speech made here in 1829. "My Country 'tis of Thee" was first sung in public here in 1831. An excellent stop for architecture lovers.

✚ J5 ✉ 1 Park Street 🕐 Jul–Aug Tue–Sat 8–3 🚇 Park Street 💷 Free

POST OFFICE SQUARE

A charming oasis, with a small café, surrounded by the Downtown area's skyscrapers. It's often filled with office workers at lunchtime, however; arrive in late morning or late afternoon to get a park bench and best appreciate the sights and sounds.

✚ K5 ✉ Between Milk and Franklin streets 🚇 State

ROBERT GOULD SHAW MEMORIAL

A sensitive bronze battle frieze by Augustus Saint-Gaudens unveiled in 1897 in honor of the Massachusetts 54th Regiment. Shaw, depicted in the film *Glory*, led the Union's first black regiment in the Civil War. Here, for the first time, African Americans were portrayed by a white artist as individuals.

✚ J5 ✉ Beacon Street, facing State House 🚇 Park Street 💷 Free

Old South Meeting House

Pausing for a rest at the base of the Robert Gould Shaw Monument

Walk This Way

The areas around Boston Common and the Waterfront are some of the most pedestrian-friendly, with historic stops and shopping.

DISTANCE: 0.8 miles (1.2km) **ALLOW:** 2–4 hours

START

BOSTON COMMON
(▷ 50) ✚ J6 🚇 Boylston

① From the Boylston T stop, walk left for about a block on Tremont Street, cross Tremont, and take your first right on Avery Street. You will pass the Ritz-Carlton on your right.

② Where Avery street ends, take a right onto Washington Street, followed by a left onto Essex Street. Follow Essex Street into Chinatown, where you could stop for a meal.

③ Two blocks down Essex Street, take a left onto Chauncy Street. Follow it to Summer Street, and take a left.

④ After one block you will hit Downtown Crossing. This is the center of bargain shopping in Boston.

END

NEW ENGLAND AQUARIUM
(▷ 53) ✚ L5 🚇 Aquarium

⑧ Across from City Hall, cross Congress Street to Faneuil Hall (▷ 26). On the other side of Faneuil Hall, cross the street to the New England Aquarium (▷ 53).

⑦ Follow Washington to State Street and take a right. Where State meets Congress Street, take a left. City Hall will be on your left.

⑥ Follow Washington to the right. Pass the Diamond District at 333 Washington—full of jewelry bargains (▷ 58).

⑤ Continue up Washington several blocks to the Old South Meeting House (▷ 56).

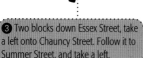

57

Shopping

BRATTLE BOOK SHOP

www.brattlebookshop.com

A treasure trove of rare and secondhand books with a good section on Boston and New England. It's been in business since the 19th century. So count on finding plenty of out-of-print and rare books, plus academic works, maps and old leather-bound books.

✚ J5 ✉ 9 West Street ☎ 617/542-0210 🚇 Park Street

BROMFIELD PEN SHOP

www.bromfieldpenshop.com

Pens, from vintage early 1900s models to new Montblanc, Cross and cheap disposables.

✚ J5 ✉ 5 Bromfield Street ☎ 617/482-9053 🚇 Park Street

DOWNTOWN CROSSING

www.downtowncrossing.org

Stores selling street fashion, shoes, jewelry, cameras and the like, plus the city's main department stores. Encompassing part of Washington, Winter and Bromfield streets, Downtown Crossing is mainly pedestrians-only.

✚ J6 🚇 Downtown Crossing

FOOT PATHS

www.footpathsshoes.com

Elegant, casual and athletic shoes for men and women, plus a full range of hiking boots.

✚ K6 ✉ 415 Washington Street ☎ 617/338-6008 🚇 Downtown Crossing

THE ICA STORE

www.icastore.org

Arguably the most exciting design gift shop in Boston, the ICA Store carries a stunning selection of jewelry, household decor items, children's toys, accessories and books on contemporary art and design.

✚ L6 ✉ 100 Northern Avenue ☎ 617/478-3104 ⏰ Tue–Wed, Sat–Sun 10–5, Thu–Fri 10–9 🚇 Courthouse

LOUISBOSTON

www.louisboston.com

Pronounced Loooeeez, LouisBoston has been the city's icon for stylish men's and women's fashion since the 19th century. In 2010, the store moved to a new location. As well as exclusive designer clothing, the

new store at Fan Pier has an apothecary, carrying exotic perfumes, creams and body lotions. Sam's, the store's café/restaurant is a great spot for lunch, dinner or brunch.

✚ M6 ✉ 60 Northern Avenue ☎ 617/262-6100 🚇 Court House

ST. JOHN BOUTIQUE

www.discoverstjohn.com

St. John was founded in 1962 by Robert and Marie Gray and now has stores all over the globe. Elegant, couture knitwear for women.

✚ H6 ✉ 292 Boylston Street ☎ 617/338-6130 🚇 Arlington

SKECHERS

www.skechers.com

Very cool men's, women's and kids' athletic shoes, boots, sneakers, sandals.

✚ J5 ✉ 417 Washington Street ☎ 617/423-0412 🚇 Downtown Crossing

THE TANNERY

www.thetannery.com

With a staff dedicated to finding the perfect fit for each and every customer's foot, this is the place to pick up both rugged outdoor shoes and casual numbers alike. Wide range of hiking boots and sneakers (Vans, Timberland, Sebago, Rockport). Also in Brattle Street and Harvard Square.

✚ H6 ✉ 711 Boylston Street ☎ 617/267-5500 🚇 Arlington

DOWNTOWN BARGAINS

Downtown Crossing, and all around Washington Street, is known as prime bargain territory for the marked-down jewelry sold at the **Diamond District** (at 333 Washington Street). Other discounts nearby: designer men's and women's shoes at DSW Shoe (385 Washington Street) and outdoor gear at Eddie Bauer Outlet (500 Washington Street).

Entertainment and Nightlife

BOSTON OPERA HOUSE

www.bostonoperahouse.com
Originally a vaudeville theater, this grand showroom was beautifully restored in 2004. It now features the biggest Broadway touring productions, as well as the Boston Ballet's annual Christmas performances of *The Nutcracker* by Tchaikovsky.

➕ K6 ✉ 539 Washington Street ☎ 617/259-3400 🚇 Chinatown, Boylston

CHARLES PLAYHOUSE

www.blueman.com
Shear Madness, a comedy whodunnit set in a hairdresser's, has played here since 1980. *Blue Man Group*, another long-running show, presents its offbeat mix of visually stunning theater, music and performance art on the Charles' other stage.

➕ J6 ✉ 74 Warrenton Street ☎ 617/426-5225 *(Shear Madness)*; 617/426-6912 *(Blue Man Group)* 🚇 Boylston

COLONIAL THEATRE

www.citicenter.org
This lush, beautifully restored, turn-of-the-19th-century theater stages pre-Broadway productions as well as a range of other performing arts events.

➕ J6 ✉ 106 Boylston Street ☎ 877/613-0134 🚇 Boylston

CUTLER MAJESTIC THEATRE

www.cutlermajestic.org
Visiting dance troupes, world music performers, Shakespearean actors and Emerson College student productions all use the stage at this 1903 venue.

➕ J6 ✉ 219 Tremont Street ☎ 617/824-8000 🚇 Boylston

DICK DOHERTY'S COMEDY DEN

www.dickdoherty.com
A leading comedy venue, beneath a lively club.

➕ J6 ✉ 184 High Street ☎ 800/401-2221 🎭 Shows daily 🚇 Aquarium

EMMANUEL CHURCH

www.emmanuelmusic.org
A Bach cantata every Sunday (Sep–May).

➕ H6 ✉ 15 Newbury Street ☎ 617/536-3356 🚇 Arlington

TICKETS

BosTix sell half-price theater tickets on the day of the show (from 11am). As a fully fledged Ticketmaster outlet, it also sells full-price tickets in advance for venues in Boston and the rest of New England. Booths are at: ✉ Faneuil Hall Marketplace 🕐 Tue–Sat 10–6, Sun 11–4; ✉ Copley Square 🕐 Mon–Sat 10–6, Sun 11–4. Tickets cover theater, concerts, museums, sports events and trolley tours. Cash and credit cards are accepted.

THE GOOD LIFE

www.goodlifebar.com
A stylish lounge offering a menu of gourmet pizzas and small plates for sharing. More than 125 varieties of vodka at the frozen vodka bar.

➕ K6 ✉ 28 Kingston Street ☎ 617/451-2622 🚇 Park, Downtown Crossing

HUB PUB

www.thehubpub.com
Close to the Theatre District, this is a busy pub serving hearty food till 1am every night of the week. Big on TV sports.

➕ K5 ✉ 18 Province Street ☎ 617/227-8952 🚇 Park

INSTITUTE OF CONTEMPORARY ART (ICA)

www.icaboston.org
An exhibition, film and performance space (▷ 52).

➕ M6 ✉ 100 Northern Avenue 🚇 Courthouse

JACQUE'S CABARET

www.jacques-cabaret.com
And now for something completely different… Female impersonators and other offbeat performances draw everyone from drag queens to bachelorette parties.

➕ J6 ✉ 79 Broadway ☎ 617/426-8902 🚇 Arlington

JM CURLEY

jmcurleyboston.com
Named for James Michael Curley, the controversial but popular mayor of

Boston, who was once re-elected while in jail, this pub has a great vibe and great pub food.

🏠 J5 ✉ 21 Temple Place ☎ 617/338-5333 🚇 Park

NICK'S COMEDY STOP

www.nickscomedystop.com
A well-loved Theater District comedy club with local stars and would-be stars on stage.

🏠 J6 ✉ 100 Warrenton Street ☎ 617/830-2551 🚇 Boylston

ROWES WHARF BAR AT BOSTON HARBOR HOTEL

www.bhh.com
Sophisticated and comfortable, Rowes Wharf Bar serves classic Boston pub fare, fine blended and single-malt scotch and serious martinis.

🏠 L5 ✉ 70 Rowes Wharf ☎ 617/439-7000 🚇 Aquarium

ROYALE BOSTON

royaleboston.com
With its edgy live bands and cutting-edge DJs, the crowded and loud Royale is Boston's No.1 megaclub, set in a vast ballroom.

🏠 J6 ✉ 279 Tremont Street ☎ 617/338-7699 🚇 Boylston, Chinatown

SCHOLARS AMERICAN BISTRO & COCKTAIL LOUNGE

www.scholarsbostonbistro.com
From electro house and retro to jazz brunches,

this central pub/cocktail bar/disco and pool hall is always humming, especially after work. Good value food is served.

🏠 K5 ✉ 25 School Street ☎ 617/248-0025 🚇 Park

SILVERTONE BAR & GRILL

www.silvertonedowntown.com
Popular subterranean joint just off the Common features comfy booths, creative martinis and a bar menu of comfort food like mac 'n' cheese and meatloaf. Crowded on weekends.

🏠 K5 ✉ 69 Bromfield Street ☎ 617/338-7887 🚇 Park Street

W LOUNGE

www.starwoodhotels.com
With its oversized chairs and sofas and cheerful fire pit, low lighting and romantic ambience, all

---

CHEAP THEATER

Productions in the Theater District can be expensive. If you are willing to roll the dice, many college theater groups offer fine productions at lower prices. For example, the **Playwright's Theatre** at Boston University (949 Commonwealth Avenue, 617/358-7529) showcases plays written or produced by students or alumni. Particularly popular is the annual **Boston Theater Marathon,** which features 50 10-minute plays every spring.

---

that is needed is the signature W cocktail. Located in the W Hotel (▷ 112).

🏠 J6 ✉ 100 Stuart Street ☎ 617/310-6790 🚇 Chinatown

THE WANG THEATRE

www.citicenter.org
A 1920s movie palace used for concerts, opera, dance and the impressive Boston Ballet (tel 617/482-9393), which performs classical and contemporary dance. The 3,600-seat theater has been renovated.

🏠 J6 ✉ 270 Tremont Street ☎ 617/482-9393 🚇 Boylston

WHISKY SAIGON

www.whiskysaigon.com
On the site of the old Gypsy Bar, this hip new hotspot features some of Boston's best DJs, as well as new Funktion One surround-sound and state-of-the-art special effects.

🏠 J6 ✉ 116 Boylston Street ☎ 617/482-7799 🚇 Boylston

THE WILBUR THEATRE

thewilbur.com
In the heart of Boston's historic Theatre District, the century-old Wilbur Theatre regularly hosts some of America's finest comedians as well as live music from stars such as Dr. John, The Temptations and Judy Collins.

🏠 J6 ✉ 246 Tremont Street ☎ 617/248-9700 🚇 Boylston

Restaurants

PRICES

Prices are approximate, based on a 3-course meal for one person.
$$$ over $40
$$ $20–$40
$ under $20

AURA ($$$)

www.aurarestaurant.com
Beautiful presentations that spotlight the inventive combinations of ingredients are the signature of Aura's imaginative chef. And the hotel's no-tipping policy applies here, too, making the prices less onerous than in other restaurants of its high caliber. Desserts are outstanding.
🚩 L6 ✉ Seaport Hotel, 1 Seaport Lane (Northern Avenue) ☎ 617/385-4300 🕐 Breakfast daily, lunch Mon–Fri, dinner Tue–Sat 🚇 World Trade Center

BARKING CRAB ($)

A rough-and-ready clam shack where you can eat indoors or alfresco, with downtown views across the water. Expect crowds, a wait, noise and fun.
🚩 L6 ✉ 88 Sleeper Street, off Northern Avenue, Waterfront ☎ 617/426-2722 🕐 From 11.30am 🚇 South Station

BISTRO DU MIDI ($$)

www.bistrodumidi.com
French Provincial cuisine served in an exceptional location overlooking the Public Garden with a street-level bar offering food and drink. There is also an upstairs Gardenview French-styled dining room with wooden beams and fireplace, as well as an outdoor patio.
🚩 H6 ✉ 272 Boylston Street, Theatre District ☎ 617/426-7878 🕐 Lunch, dinner daily 🚇 Arlington

THE BRISTOL LOUNGE ($$$)

www.fourseasons.com/boston/dining
Overlooking the Public Garden and known as much for the service as the food, this is one of Boston's best formal restaurants. Upscale comfort food, including the Bristol Burger, homemade pasta and fresh seafood.
🚩 J6 ✉ Four Seasons Hotel (▷ 112), 200 Boylston Street ☎ 617/351-2037

(▷ 112)

PEOPLE-WATCHING

Some of the best restaurants are also the sites of its best people-watching scenes. On Boston Common, eateries like Bistro du Midi and Via Matta invite you to survey the weekend strolls taken by crowds in the verdant Public Garden. In the South End, colorful hordes of people walk the sidewalks outside bistros like Hamersley's and Union Bar & Grille. But for the most eclectic sightings, go to Newbury Street, where the outdoor cafés are perfectly perched.

🕐 Breakfast, lunch, dinner daily 🚇 Arlington

CAFÉ FLEURI ($$)

Bright and open, with well-spaced tables, this smart atrium café specializes in dishes created to showcase seasonal local ingredients. The Saturday Chocolate Bar is a decadent buffet of chocolate desserts.
🚩 K5 ✉ The Langham Boston, 250 Franklin Street ☎ 617/956-8751 🕐 Breakfast and lunch daily 🚇 Downtown Crossing

CHAU CHOW CITY ($$)

Traditional dim sum midday meals are a favorite here, served from carts loaded with steaming buns filled with pork or bean paste, dumplings with meat, shrimp or vegetables and a variety of desserts. Every day has something different, with weekends featuring the largest selection.
🚩 J6 ✉ 83 Essex Street ☎ 617/338-8158 🕐 Lunch, dinner daily 🚇 Chinatown

ESPRESSO LOVE ($)

www.espressolove.com
The city version of a Martha's Vineyard favorite, serving great coffee and freshly baked blueberry muffins and breads, as well as soups and sandwiches.
🚩 K5 ✉ 33 Broad Street ☎ 857/284-7462 🕐 Daily 6.30–6; lunch 11–4 🚇 State/Aquarium

GRILL 23 & BAR ($$$)

www.grill23.com

Steaks, prime rib of beef, lamb chops, swordfish and more. Attentive service in a men's club-style room.

✚ H6 ✉ 161 Berkeley Street (at Stuart Street)
☎ 617/542-2255 ⏰ Dinner daily 🚇 Arlington

LTK BAR AND KITCHEN ($$)

www.ltkbarandkitchen.com

A modern and daring offshoot of the Legal Sea Foods chain, this outpost serves up crunchy, corn-meal-fried clams and spicy Asian lobster. Ask to borrow one of the iPod docks on offer and you can have your own personal jukebox at your table.

✚ L6 ✉ 225 Northern Avenue ☎ 617/330-7430
⏰ Lunch, dinner daily (till late) 🚇 South Station

MARLIAVE ($$–$$$)

marliave.com

The osso buco and risotto, onion soup and escargots reflect the menu's French and Italian inspiration, but there are familiar American favorites, with pastrami and Reuben sandwiches. Breads are made inhouse, along with desserts, sauces, pasta and ice cream. At the raw bar, check out the $1 "happy hour" for local oysters and clams, 4–6 and 9–10 daily.

✚ J5 ✉ 10 Bosworth Street ☎ 617/422-0004 ⏰ Daily 11–10 🚇 Park

MERITAGE ($$$)

www.meritagetherestaurant.com

A feast for the eyes as well as the palate, dining at Meritage combines a quartet of superlatives: cuisine, wine pairings, service and harbor view.

✚ L5 ✉ 70 Rowes Wharf ☎ 617/439-3995
⏰ Dinner daily, breakfast Sun 🚇 Aquarium

NEW JUMBO SEAFOOD ($)

www.newjumboseafoodrestaurant.com

Crowds flock to this enclave of superlative Chinese food for the superfresh, water tank-straight-to-wok shrimp, lobster and flounder dishes. Try giant clams in blackbean sauce.

✚ J6 ✉ 5 Hudson Street ☎ 617/542-2823 ⏰ Lunch, dinner daily 🚇 Chinatown

---

FOR VEGETARIANS

More and more restaurants include at least one entrée, and many will make up a vegetarian plate on request. In Chinatown try **My Thai Vegan Café** (✉ 3 Beach Street ☎ 617/451-2395). There is sophisticated vegetarian fare Downtown. Try **Milk Street Café** (✉ 50 Milk Street, Financial District ☎ 617/542-3663), a vegetarian-kosher luncheon-ette selling salads, soups and vegetable sandwiches, plus meatless entrées.

NEW SHANGHAI ($)

www.bostonnewshanghai.com

Upscale Chinatown eatery, specializing in Shanghai-style cuisine. Cold appetizers such as eggplant with garlic sauce.

✚ J6 ✉ 21 Hudson Street ☎ 617/338-6688 ⏰ Lunch, dinner daily 🚇 Chinatown

ROWES WHARF SEA GRILLE ($$)

www.roweswharfseagrille.com

Boston Harbor Hotel's waterside bar-restaurant and patio is one of the town's finest casual options—for both its top-notch shrimp cocktail and its breezy, flower-festooned outdoor patio.

✚ L5 ✉ 70 Rowes Wharf ☎ 617/856-7744
⏰ Breakfast, lunch, afternoon tea, dinner daily 🚇 Aquarium

TEATRO ($$–$$$)

www.teatroboston.com

A beautiful, blue-lit boîte filled with theater-going crowds in for the authentic Italian menu.

✚ J6 ✉ 177 Tremont Street, Downtown ☎ 617/778-6841
⏰ Dinner Tue–Sun 🚇 Park Street

VIA MATTA ($$)

www.viamattarestaurant.com

Step into this chic, noisy dining room for simple but extremely fresh Italian specialties. In warm weather, make for the pretty, patio dining area.

✚ H6 ✉ 79 Park Plaza ☎ 617/422-0008 ⏰ Lunch Mon–Fri, dinner Mon–Sat. Closed Sun 🚇 Arlington

Home to some of the finest shopping and people-watching in all the city, Back Bay and the South End are also vibrant residential neighborhoods.

Sights	**66–78**	
Walk	**79**	
Shopping	**80–81**	
Entertainment and Nightlife	**82–83**	
Restaurants	**84**	

Top 25 **TOP 25**

Boston Public Library ▷ **66**
Commonwealth Avenue ▷ **67**
Isabella Stewart Gardner Museum ▷ **68**
Museum of Fine Arts ▷ **70**
Newbury Street ▷ **72**
Prudential Center and Skywalk ▷ **73**
The South End ▷ **74**
Trinity Church and Copley Square ▷ **76**

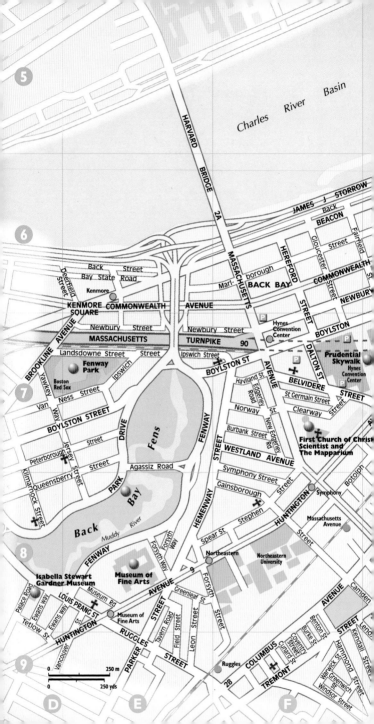

5

Charles River Basin

HARVARD BRIDGE 2A

JAMES J STORROW

BEACON

Back

Street

Fairfield

Street

6

Gloucester Street

HEREFORD STREET

COMMONWEALTH

Back

Street

Bay State Road

Marl-borough

BACK BAY

NEWBURY

Deerfield Street

MASSACHUSETTS AVENUE

Kenmore

KENMORE SQUARE

COMMONWEALTH

AVENUE

BOYLSTON

Newbury Street

Newbury Street

Hynes Convention Center

DALTON ST

Prudential Skywalk

MASSACHUSETTS

TURNPIKE

90

Hynes Convention Center

BROOKLINE AVENUE

Landsdowne Street

Ipswich Street

BOYLSTON ST

BELVIDERE STREET

Fenway Park

Haviland St

Edgerley Road

St Germain Street

Boston Red Sox

7

Yawkey Way

Ipswich Street

Norway

St

New Edgerley Rd

Clearway Street

First Church of Christ Scientist and The Mapparium

Van Ness Street

Burbank Street

BOYLSTON STREET

Street

FENWAY STREET

WESTLAND AVENUE

Jersey Street

PARK DRIVE

Fens

Symphony Street

HUNTINGTON

Symphony

Botolph Street

Peterborough Street

Queensberry Street

Agassiz Road

Gainsborough Street

Massachusetts Avenue

Kilmarnock Street

Back Bay

Muddy River

HEMENWAY STREET

Stephen Street

Spear St

8

FENWAY

Forsyth Way

Forsyth Street

Northeastern

Northeastern University

AVENUE

Isabella Stewart Gardner Museum

Museum of Fine Arts

Greenleaf St

9

Palace Road

LOUIS PRANG ST

Museum Rd

Museum of Fine Arts

Tavern Road

Field Street

Leon Street

AVENUE

Camden Street

Evans Way

Tetlow Street

HUNTINGTON

Evans Way

RUGGLES STREET

PARKER STREET

COLUMBUS AVENUE

Ruggles

28

TREMONT

Leno Street

Kendall Street

Windsor Street

Greenwich Street

Hammond Street

Warwick Street

Coventry Street

Burke St

Benton St

Cunard St

Cunard St

Vancouver Street

0   250 m

0   250 yds

D   E   F

MEMORIAL DRIVE

Charles River Esplanade

EMBANKMENT ROAD

Charles River Embankment
Storrow Lagoon

Gibson House Museum

BERKELEY

Street

STREET

EXETER

Marlborough

Street

DARTMOUTH STREET

Copley Theater

CLARENDON STREET

BERKELEY STREET

Commonwealth Avenue

AVENUE

2

STREET

Providence Street

AVENUE

Newbury Street

STREET

Trinity Church and Copley Square

Copley

JAMES ST

Lyric Stage

STREET

Hancock Tower

Stuart

Street

28

Boston Public Library

Back Bay/ South End

CLARENDON

AVENUE

Prudential Center

DARTMOUTH

BERKELEY

BACK BAY STATION

COLUMBUS

STREET

Prudential

Harcourt St.

9

Garrison St.

CHANDLER STREET

Lawrence St.

Street

AVENUE

Yarmouth Street

West

STREET

Appleton Street

Gray Street

Braddock Parkway

Holyoke Street

STREET

Gray Street

Avenue

Boston Center for the Arts

NEWTON

Durham Street

W.

Rutland Square

GREENWICH

AVENUE

Warren Avenue

Canton Street

Warren

Montgomery

TREMONT STREET

Dwight Street

Milford Street

Hanson Street

Waltham

Bradford St.

Claremont Pk.

CONCORD SQUARE

Worcester

COLUMBUS

Rutland Square

STREET

Pembroke Street

West Brookline Street

Street

DEDHAM STREET

Union Pk. Street

AVENUE

Union Park

STREET

Springfield

TREMONT

WEST CONCORD

Rutland Street

Street

SHAWMUT STREET

WASHINGTON

MONSIGNOR REYNOLDS WAY

AVENUE

Street

MALDEN ST

MASSACHUSETTS

AVENUE

STREET

STREET

SOUTH END

HARRISON

Plympton Street

Waltham Street

Northampton

AVENUE

Blackstone Square

Franklin Square

East Street

E Dedham Street

E Canton Street

STREET

SHAWMUT

Street

WASHINGTON

EAST NEWTON

St George

EAST CONCORD

Worcester Square

AVENUE

East Brookline Street

AVENUE

HARRISON STREET

ALBANY STREET

Ramsey Park

G

H

Boston Public Library

The illuminated marble staircase (left) and cloisters (right)

THE BASICS

www.bpl.org

G6

Copley Square

617/536-5400

Mon–Thu 9–9, Fri–Sat 9–5; Oct–May Sun 1–5

Nearby

Copley

Good

Free

Tours (Dartmouth Street entrance) Mon 2.30, Tue, Thu 6, Fri–Sat 11; also Sun 2 (Oct–May only). Lectures

HIGHLIGHTS

● Puvis de Chavannes murals
● John Singer Sargent murals
● Daniel Chester French bronze doors
● The courtyard

TIP

● Free lunchtime concerts in the courtyard on Fridays in the summer.

This is no ordinary library. Behind its granite facade lies an opulent institution built in Renaissance palazzo style and decorated with sculptures and paintings by some of the best artists of the day.

The education of the people A people's palace dedicated to the advancement of learning was what Charles Follen McKim was commissioned to design. An architectural landmark in the classical style, facing H. H. Richardson's Romanesque Trinity Church across Copley Square, it opened its doors to the public in 1895. It is now the Research Library, the General Library being housed in the adjoining 1972 Johnson Building.

Further treasures Pass between Bela Pratt's voluptuous bronzes, *Science* and *Art* (1912), to enter through Daniel Chester French's bronze doors. Ascend the marble staircase, guarded by lions by Louis Saint-Gaudens (Augustus's brother), and from its windows catch a glimpse of the peaceful courtyard. The stairs and landing are decorated with panels by Puvis de Chavannes, whimsical representations of the muses of inspiration. The Abbey Room has paintings depicting the quest for the Holy Grail, by Edwin Austin Abbey. Bates Hall is a magnificent room; get a close-up view of its highly decorative, barrel-vaulted ceiling from the stairs that lead up to the Sargent Gallery. The John Singer Sargent murals, *Triumph of Religion*, completed in 1919, were restored in 2004. Pause to sit in the colonnaded courtyard, watching the fountain and enjoying the tranquility.

Commonwealth Avenue

A Parisian-style boulevard lined with the grandest houses in Boston is at the heart of an amazing piece of 19th-century urban planning. To walk down it is to be transported to a different age.

Landfill By the 1850s, Boston was getting over-crowded. Desperate for land, developers turned to the swampy "back bay" of the Charles River, embarking on a remarkable landfill project to create a new residential district. Inspired by Paris's boulevard system, the architect Arthur Gilman planned a grid, eight blocks long and four blocks wide, with a long central mall.

Commonwealth Avenue Even the nouveau-riche industrialists who flocked to the Back Bay felt some of the Puritan restraints of the Proper Bostonians of Beacon Hill, and their rows of ostentatious brownstones are a somewhat subdued blend of Victorian styles. The centerpiece is Commonwealth Avenue. Central gardens are lined with trees; in spring magnolias bloom in profusion. The Boston Women's Memorial lies between Fairfield and Gloucester streets. Most houses are now apartments, some are offices. The châteaulike Burrage Mansion at Hereford Street stands out, with statuettes everywhere. To see inside a more average home, visit Gibson House Museum on Beacon Street.

Feeling fit? The mall is just part of a 7-mile (11km) long "Emerald Necklace" of green space stretching from Boston Common to Franklin Park.

THE BASICS

➕ G6
🍴 Newbury and Boylston streets
🚇 Arlington, Copley, Hynes Convention Center

HIGHLIGHTS

● Magnolias in spring on Commonwealth Avenue
● Lights on the mall at Christmas
● Memorial to firemen killed in the Hotel Vendome fire

TIPS

● More intimate than Commonwealth Avenue and no less beautiful is next-door Marlborough Street, which is lined with flowering dogwoods in the springtime.
● North–south streets are named alphabetically, Arlington to Hereford.

Isabella Stewart Gardner Museum

HIGHLIGHTS

● Renzo Piano's new (2012) wing provides a restaurant, greenhouses and more; the palazzo is as it was a century ago

TIPS

● In some of the rooms you must pull back curtains and open drawers to see the priceless objects that are protected from the light.
● If your first name is Isabella, congratulations—you get free admission to the museum.

The woman who created this collection of "beautiful things" had a passion for art, music and horticulture. Her finds are arranged in a Venetian-style house built around a flower-filled courtyard.

"Beautiful things" Determined to give her country world-class art, Mrs Gardner made a start in 1896 by buying a Rembrandt self-portrait. Her collection grew to include work by Vermeer, Giotto, Botticelli, Raphael, Degas and Matisse, as well as John Singer Sargent and James McNeill Whistler. She also bought prints and drawings, books, sculptures, ceramics and glass, tapestries, carpets, lace, stained glass, ironwork and furniture.

Music and horticulture The building itself, known as Fenway Court, and the atmosphere

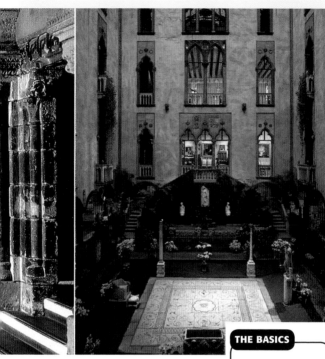

El Jaleo *by John Singer Sargent in the Spanish Cloister of the Isabella Stewart Gardner Museum (left); the interior facade that overlooks the courtyard, which is filled with planting and statuary (right)*

that pervades it, is as much the creation of Mrs Gardner as her collection. She arranged her objects in a series of rooms—the Raphael Room, the Titian Room, the Gothic Room, the intimate Blue Room and more. She filled the courtyard with sculptures, plants and trees, and she celebrated the opening of her home (she lived on the top floor) to the public with a concert given by members of the Boston Symphony Orchestra. Today, concerts are held in the Tapestry Room on Sundays from September to May.

Art heist The collection suffered a terrible loss—and America's biggest art theft—in March 1990 when thieves dressed as policemen made off with 13 items, which have not been recovered. Among them were a priceless Vermeer and *The Sea of Galilee,* Rembrandt's only seascape.

THE BASICS

www.gardnermuseum.org
🚇 D8
✉ 280 The Fenway
☎ 617/566-1401
🕐 Wed–Mon 11–5 (Thu till 8.30). Closed Tue except most public hols
🍴 On premises
🚉 Museum of Fine Arts
♿ Good
💷 Expensive
❓ Concerts: Sep–May Sun 1.30 (☎ 617/278-5156). Courtyard: talks most weekdays (times posted at the information desk). Audio tours $4. Lectures, shop

Museum of Fine Arts

TOP 25

The MFA is one of America's foremost museums. The Asian collection is unrivaled in this hemisphere, the European art is superb and the American rooms are excellent. If time is limited, take a guided tour of the highlights.

Asian, Egyptian, Classical The MFA's Nubian collection is the best outside the Sudan. It is all exquisite, from the neat rows of little *shawabtis* (figurines) to the faience jewelry. The Egyptian rooms are popular, with mummies, hieroglyphics and splendid Old Kingdom sculptures. Buddhist sculptures, Chinese ceramics and Indian paintings make up part of an Asian collection.

European In the European galleries, seek out the little gem of a Rembrandt in a glass case,

Huntington Staircase in the museum (left); Cyrus Dallin's 1909 statue Appeal to the Great Spirit *stands at the entrance to the museum (right)*

then take in works of Tiepolo, Gainsborough, Turner, Delacroix, Constable and a good number of Millets. The Impressionist room is an array of familiar paintings, with works from Monet and Renoir to Gauguin. There is porcelain from all over Europe and period rooms from Britain.

American The spectacular Art of the Americas wing showcases more than 5,000 works of art from South, Central and North America. The collection includes art in all media displayed chronologically in 53 galleries, beginning with ancient Mayan ceramics through the late 20th-century art of Jackson Pollack. There are also major pieces of silver by Paul Revere, portraits by John Singleton Copley and John Singer Sargent and landscapes by Georgia O'Keeffe. Furniture and decorative arts are featured in nine period rooms.

THE BASICS

www.mfa.org
✚ E8
✉ 465 Huntington Avenue
☎ 617/267-9300
🕐 Mon–Tue 10–4.45, Wed–Fri 10–9.45, Sat–Sun 10–4.45
🍴 Choice on premises
🚇 Museum of Fine Arts
♿ Excellent
💲 Expensive. Wed 4–9.45 voluntary contribution. Boston CityPass applies
❓ Regular free guided tours Mon–Sat. Film programs Thu–Sun. Lectures, concerts. Good shop

Newbury Street

TOP 25

Newbury Street houses retail and residential buildings (left and right)

Newbury Street is the place to go if you are interested in buying artwork—paintings, prints or sculpture. But art isn't the only draw at Boston's answer to Paris's Champs-Élysées.

Galleries Many a pleasant hour can be spent browsing in the galleries, stopping off in a café now and then. Individual small shops are housed in beautiful historic row houses (terraces). A concentration of galleries lies between Arlington and Fairfield streets. They display works by 19th- and 20th-century artists, in addition to contemporary pieces. The Robert Klein Gallery, at 38 Newbury Street, is the only major art gallery in New England dedicated to fine art photography. If you are interested in avant-garde galleries explore the South End, particularly around Harrison and Thayer streets.

Shop, shop, shop Shopping is also an enormous draw of the area. At the intersection with Arlington Street, where shops tend to be high-end and high-priced, shoppers find plenty of international jewelry shops, fashion designers and day spas. That stable gives way to more mid-range shops as you move toward the other end of the street, which intersects with Massachusetts Avenue. On the way there, cross mainstream fashion chains, gift shops, independent boutiques and hair salons. One thing the entire street lays claim to, however, is an abundance of cafés and restaurants. Duck into any with an outdoor patio to get a first-rate spot for people-watching.

THE BASICS

www.newbury-st.com

⊞ G6

✉ Between Arlington Street and Massachusetts Avenue

🕐 Most shops open 10–6

🍴 Excellent bistros line each side of the street

🚇 Arlington, Copley, Massachusetts Avenue

♿ Fair to excellent, depending on the business. Many have elevators

HIGHLIGHTS

● Window-shopping in Newbury Street
● People-watching in the Newbury Street cafés
● At 39 Newbury Street, Shreve, Crump & Low is America's oldest jeweler (established 1796)

The view from the tower at night (left); retail outlets (middle); the Prudential Tower (right)

 TOP 25

Prudential Center and Skywalk

An architecturally unremarkable building offers bird's-eye views of Boston and the New England countryside from its 50th floor. Drop back closer to the ground for shops and eating places.

Skywalk at the Prudential The Prudential Tower is architecturally undistinguished, part of the 1960s Prudential Center office and shopping complex. But take the elevator to the Skywalk on the 50th floor and you have stunning 360-degree views—weather permitting, as far as the mountains of New Hampshire. Pick out the gold dome of the State House; peer down onto the rooftops of the neat Back Bay homes and over the Charles River to MIT and Cambridge; see the parks of the "Emerald Necklace" stretching into the distance; look out to the Boston Harbor Islands. Interactive exhibits cover key historical and sporting events, as well as distinguished buildings and residents. Looking to relax while soaking up that same stunning view? The Top of the Hub restaurant, on the Pru's 52nd floor, looks out to the twinkling city and beyond; be sure to stop in for a cocktail or dessert, and a city profile you won't soon forget.

Down to earth Meanwhile, on the lower levels of the building, find plenty of indoor shopping and snacking. The food courtyard caters to diners-in-a-rush with chain cafés and several more sedate sit-down establishments, while the stores lure shoppers in for high-end jewelry, international fashions, quality stationery and flowers.

THE BASICS

www.skywalkboston.com
➕ G7
✉ Prudential Tower, 800 Boylston Street
☎ 617/859-0648
🕐 Daily 10–10. Skywalk: Mar–Oct 10–9.30, Nov–Feb 10–8
🍴 Top of the Hub; choice in Prudential Center
Ⓣ Prudential, Hynes Convention Center
♿ Excellent
✋ Expensive. Boston CityPass applies

HIGHLIGHTS

● Views from the Pru after snow
● Views from the Pru at night
● Top of the Hub bar and restaurant on the 52nd floor
● Sushi at Haru (▷ 84), outside the Huntington Avenue entrance
● Live jazz nightly in the Top of the Hub lounge

BACK BAY AND THE SOUTH END TOP 25

73

The South End

HIGHLIGHTS

● Excellent bistros and restaurants in Tremont and Washington streets
● Cutting-edge art galleries, trendy gift shops and home stores

TIPS

● Be sure to make a reservation before visiting the area's restaurants: tables fill up fast.
● Dog lovers shouldn't miss the residential blocks' small hidden parks, where canines and their owners congregate nightly.

First occupied by musicians and teachers in the 1850s, the South End had taken a social nose-dive by the end of the 19th century but is now very much back in vogue with young professionals and artists.

Residential It is a lively residential area, whose elegant bow-fronted terraces, many profusely decorated with balustrades and window boxes, line leafy streets and squares. Running through the middle is Tremont Street, where local shops are punctuated by trendy places to eat. There is a broad ethnic mix here and a strong gay community. The South End has a growing number of art galleries, particularly around Harrison and Thayer streets. The neighborhood lies between Huntington Avenue and the Expressway.

The South End's Victorian houses (left and right)

So Wa'? The most rapidly changing area of the South End is the SoWa district (so named because it sits South of Washington Street). Blessed with the hottest new restaurants and cafés—from Union Bar & Grille to Flour Bakery (both ▷ 84)—the area currently has some of the most expensive real estate and most adventurous interior design in the city, but it has still not been entirely gentrified (a fact that locals say lends it an urbane, gritty feel).

By day and by night Walk the neighborhood's parks during the day, admire its rooftops and the tiny gardens in front of its brownstones, visit its trendy art galleries and home goods shops, then stay to enjoy dinner in its stylish restaurants. Spring and summer bring elaborate gardens into bloom and fine alfresco dining.

THE BASICS

www.south-end-boston.com

➕ H8

✉ Between the Greenway and Massachusetts Avenue

🕐 Most shops open 10–6. Most restaurants open 5pm–midnight

🍴 Excellent bistros line each side of the street

🚇 Back Bay Station, New England Medical Center

♿ Fair to excellent, depending on the business. Many have elevators

Trinity Church and Copley Square

HIGHLIGHTS

Trinity Church
● Polychrome interior
● John La Farge paintings and lancet windows
● Lantern tower
● Christmas candlelight services

TIP

● Free guided tours of Trinity Church are offered most days. Call for schedule.

H. H. Richardson's prototype French Romanesque church is often described as America's masterpiece of ecclesiastical architecture. It faces Copley Square, bounded by other notable buildings—Boston Public Library and the Fairmont Copley Plaza Hotel.

Trinity Church The Back Bay was a newly developed landfill area when in 1872 Henry Hobson Richardson was commissioned to draw up designs for a new Trinity Church. A massive lantern tower over the transept crossing dominates the church inside and out, requiring more than 2,000 wooden piles massed together to support its granite foundations. Externally, the granite blocks are broken up by bands of pink sandstone. Inside, John La Farge created an

Trinity Church sits alongside its tall neighbor, reflected in the mirrorlike glass (left); detail of the ornate frescos by John La Farge that decorate the walls above the gilded archway in Trinity Church (middle); the contrasting 19th-century and 20th-century architecture (right)

intricate polychrome interior, a tapestry of reds and greens highlighted with gold. The church also contains several important examples of La Farge's ground-breaking stained-glass work. In the baptistery is a bust by Daniel Chester French of the portly rector Phillips Brooks, who composed the carol "O Little Town of Bethlehem."

John Hancock Tower There is something immensely serene about this icy shaft of blue glass. Designed by Henry Cobb, of I. M. Pei & Partners, the building caused a big sensation at first. But it has long since found a place in (most) Bostonians' hearts. After 9/11, the observatory on the 60th floor was closed to the public, for security reasons. But visitors can still admire the tower from the outside, walking around it to see how clearly it reflects the historic buildings nearby.

THE BASICS

Trinity Church
www.trinitychurchboston.
org
➕ G6
✉ Copley Square
☎ 617/536-0944
🕐 Daily 8–6
🚇 Copley
♿ Good
✋ Free
❓ Free half-hour organ recitals Fri 12.15. Sun services 7.45, 9, 11.15 (with choir music), 6

John Hancock Tower
➕ H6
✉ Copley Square
🍴 Nearby
🚇 Copley

More to See

BACK BAY FENS

Once a saltwater bay, this was the first of Frederick Law Olmsted's string of parks, part of the so-called "Emerald Necklace" of open green spaces. Tall rushes line the banks of the Muddy River behind the Museum of Fine Arts; stroll through the willows or sit in the Rose Garden.

☒ E8 ✉ The Fenway/Park Drive 🚇 Hynes Convention Center, Museum of Fine Arts

CHARLES RIVER ESPLANADE

A favorite for roller blading, jogging, sunbathing, boating and biking. Free summer concerts in Hatch Shell (▷ 83). Also open-air film screenings. Boat tours leave from near the Science Museum.

☒ H5 ✉ Storrow Memorial Drive 🚇 Charles/MGH

FENWAY PARK FOR RED SOX

www.redsox.com

The Boston Red Sox play from April through October. "Friendly Fenway," famous for its Green Monster, the high left-field wall, is the oldest ballpark in the US, although it has been renovated.

☒ E7 ✉ 4 Yawkey Way ☎ Tickets: 877/733-7699. Tours: 617/226-6666 🚇 Kenmore

FIRST CHURCH OF CHRIST, SCIENTIST AND THE MAPPARIUM

www.tfccs.com

www.marybakereddylibrary.org

The scale of this complex is mind-blowing. The world headquarters for the Church of Christ, Scientist, occupies 4 acres (6ha) of prime Back Bay land, with a church seating 3,000. The Mother Church of Christian Science was founded in Boston in 1892 by Mary Baker Eddy. The Mapparium, on the first floor of the Mary Baker Eddy Library, is a brightly colored stained-glass globe, so huge you can walk inside it and stand at the center of the world. It was made in the early 1930s.

☒ F7 ✉ 175 Huntington Avenue; Library: 200 Massachusetts Avenue ☎ 617/450-2000 🕐 Church: daily. Library: Tue–Sun 10–4 🚇 Prudential 👢 Library: moderate

A floodlighted Red Sox baseball game at Fenway Park

South End Stroll

You will see Victorian architecture, boutiques, restaurants and parks. Make sure you leave time to stop, browse and snack.

DISTANCE: 1.6 miles (2.5km) **ALLOW:** 3–6 hours

START

DARTMOUTH STREET
➕ G7 🚇 Back Bay Station

1 From Back Bay Station, walk several blocks down Dartmouth Street, crossing Columbus Avenue, taking note of the brick sidewalks and brownstone buildings on Chandler and Appleton streets.

2 Continue down Dartmouth to Tremont Street and turn left. On the left are the Boston Center for the Arts (▷ 82), and local institution Hamersley's Bistro (▷ 84).

3 Across Tremont, find much-loved restaurants such as B&G Oysters and the Butcher Shop (▷ 84).

4 From the Butcher Shop, take a left, returning down Tremont and pass gift shops and bistros such as Aquitaine and Metropolis.

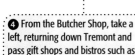

END

MASSACHUSETTS AVENUE
➕ F8 🚇 Massachusetts Avenue

8 Walk three blocks past Columbus Avenue and follow South End mall, a flower-filled walkway to the left, until it meets Massachusetts Avenue.

7 You're now in the South End's trendiest section, full of new restaurants, galleries and stores. Return on Washington, passing restaurants like Union Bar & Grille (▷ 84), and stores like Lekker (▷ 81). Next take a right on West Concord Street.

6 Continue down West Brookline, passing Blackstone Square, a small neighborhood park. When you reach Washington Street, take a left.

5 Where Tremont crosses West Brookline Street, take a left.

BACK BAY AND THE SOUTH END WALK

Shopping

ALAN BILZERIAN
www.alanbilzerian.com
A fun one for window-shopping for the latest clothes from Rick Owens, Yohji Yamamoto etc.
H6 ✉ 34 Newbury Street
☎ 617/536-1001 🚇 Arlington

ALLEN EDMONDS
www.allenedmonds.com
Top-quality shoes in classic styles come in a wide range of sizes.
H6 ✉ 36 Newbury Street
☎ 617/247-3363 🚇 Arlington

AMERICAN APPAREL
www.americanapparel.net
American Apparel is a leader in the anti-sweatshop movement. Look for all the basics here, with styles that are fun and attractive. Also carries organic clothing.
G6 ✉ 138 Newbury Street ☎ 617/236-1636
🚇 Arlington

BARNEYS NEW YORK
www.barneys.com
A second home to the city's high-spending hipsters, where you can find of-the-moment labels like 3.1 by Philip Lim and Lanvin. Don't miss the luxurious shoe section anchored by a fireplace.
G7 ✉ 100 Huntington Avenue 🚇 617/385-3300
🚇 Copley

BEAD + FIBER
www.beadandfiber.net
With its array of yarns and beads, this colorful shop is an inspiration for artists and beginners alike. Very lively during the SOWA Artists Guild First Fridays (5–9, year round).
J8 ✉ 460 Harrison Avenue ☎ 617/426-2323
🚇 Back Bay/South End

BROOKSTONE
www.brookstone.com
Household, personal and travel equipment here goes well beyond the definition of "gadgets"—they're useful, high-quality tools for living that you never knew existed.
G7 ✉ 100 Huntington Place ☎ 617/267-4308
🚇 Copley

COCO BABY
www.cocobabyboston.com
Catering to zero to 6-year-olds, this classy baby and toddler boutique features eco-conscious American and European labels.
H8 ✉ 1636 Washington Street ☎ 617/247-2229
🚇 Symphony

MORE CHOICE

These large outdoor activity stores cover every sports interest.

Eastern Mountain Sports
Hiking, backpacking, camping, mountaineering, cross-country skiing.
✉ 1041 Commonwealth Avenue ☎ 617/254-4250

City Sports
Shoes and heart-rate monitors, cycling, tennis and swimming gear. Check out the sales.
✉ 480 Boylston Street
☎ 617/267-3900

CRUSH BOUTIQUE
www.shopcrushboutique.com
This hip store offers temptation after temptation from tops, sweaters and sequined mini-dresses to fun jewelry, denim and tailored jackets. Also at 131 Charles Street.
F6 ✉ 264 Newbury Street
☎ 617/424-0010 🚇 Hynes

EMPORIO ARMANI
www.armani.com
Slightly less haute couture but more accessible price-wise than Giorgio Armani (No. 22 Newbury Street). The store has a popular café, with outside tables in summer.
G6 ✉ 2 Copley Place
☎ 617/262-7300 🚇 Copley

FLOCK BOUTIQUE
www.flockboston.com
This store concentrates on informal but snazzy easy-to-wear clothes: from dresses and sweaters to hats and fingerless mittens, unusual shoes and jewelry.
H8 ✉ 274 Shawmut Avenue ☎ 617/391-0222
🚇 Back Bay

GIFTED
www.madebymarie.com
As well as creating her own jewelry, pottery and photographs, Marie Corcoran shares her crafts store with local talent. Find fun baby clothes alongside sophisticated silk ties.
H8 ✉ 2 Dartmouth Street ☎ 617/716-9924
🚇 Back Bay

GOORIN BROS
www.goorin.com
If you like hats, you'll love Goorin Bros: hats for men, for women, for work and play, for kids. Fedoras and flat caps, beanies and bowlers.
✚ G6 ✉ 130 Newbury Street ☎ 617/247-4287 🚇 Copley

LEKKER
www.lekkerhome.com
This South End store sells unique European home accessories and furniture.
✚ G9 ✉ 1313 Washington Street ☎ 617/542-6464 🚇 Union Park Street

LIFE IS GOOD
www.lifeisgood.com
Witty bags, socks, hats and more branded with the Life is Good logo.
✚ F6 ✉ 285 Newbury Street ☎ 617/262-5068 🚇 Hynes

LUSH
www.lushusa.com
Handmade soaps and other earth-kind cosmetics are bright, unusual, nicely packaged and reasonably priced.
✚ G6 ✉ 166 Newbury Street ☎ 617/375-5874 🚇 Copley

MARC JACOBS
www.marcjacobs.com
The celebrated American designer showcases his more expensive and casual lines at this boutique. Find women's coats, dresses, pants (trousers) and skirts, plus accessories and home decor.

✚ G6 ✉ 81 Newbury Street ☎ 617/425-0707 🚇 Copley

NEWBURY COMICS
www.newburycomics.com
The hippest record shop in town. CDs, T-shirts, posters and comics.
✚ G6 ✉ 332 Newbury Street ☎ 617/236-4930 🚇 Hynes Convention Center

NIKETOWN
www.nike.com
Large, state-of-the-art store, arranged by pavilion: men's and women's shoes for training and running, golf, basketball, soccer, tennis and more.
✚ G6 ✉ 200 Newbury Street ☎ 617/267-3400 🚇 Copley

PRUDENTIAL CENTER
www.prudentialcenter.com
A dozen clothes stores (including Chico's, Ann Taylor, J.Jill and Olympia

> **INDEPENDENT SHOPS**
>
> Amid Boston's many national and international chain stores, you'll find plenty of homegrown and family-run boutiques and specialty shops. How to best find them? When walking on Newbury Street, look up. The second, third and fourth floors of the street's Victorian brownstone buildings are favorite spaces for those with less money to burn on front-and-center retail space, but with plenty of interesting and unique wares to sell.

Sports), some shoe and accessories shops, gift and specialty stores (such as Crane's stationery) and a hardware store. Also home to department stores Saks Fifth Avenue and Lord & Taylor, a post office, ATMs, a food court and Legal Sea Foods.
✚ G7 ✉ Between Boylston Street and Huntington Avenue ⏰ Mon–Sat 10–9, Sun 11–6 🚇 Prudential

SECOND TIME AROUND
www.secondtimearound.net
Not your usual thrift shop, this resale store specializes in better brands and higher quality. But it's more accessible than the traditional Junior League designer resale shops.
✚ G6 ✉ 176 Newbury Street ☎ 617/247-3504 🚇 Copley

SIMON PEARCE
www.simonpearce.com
Exquisite handmade art glass and utilitarian glassware beautiful enough to be decorator pieces. Simon Pearce is a well-known New England artist.
✚ G6 ✉ 103 Newbury Street ☎ 617/450-8388 🚇 Arlington

WILLIAMS-SONOMA
www.williams-sonoma.com
For the cook who has everything—or so you thought until you came in here: from Dualit toasters and heart-shaped muffin baking trays to French table linens.
✚ G7 ✉ Copley Place ☎ 617/262-3080 🚇 Copley

Entertainment and Nightlife

BERKLEE PERFORMANCE CENTER

www.berklee.edu/bpc

This Back Bay venue with state-of-the-art sound and lighting systems seats 1,220 and hosts jazz, pop, folk and world music concerts by international performers and by the students and staff of the Berklee College of Music.

✚ F7 ✉ 136 Massachusetts Avenue ☎ 617/747–2261 🚇 Hynes Convention Center

BLEACHER BAR

www.bleacherbarboston.com

The ultimate sports bar inside Fenway Park's Green Monster. Small and crowded at game time, the field-level view looks across centerfield to home plate. Basic beer and pub food, but the view is the real star here.

✚ E7 ✉ 82 Lansdowne Street ☎ 617/262-2424 🚇 Kenmore

BOSTON BEER WORKS

www.beerworks.net

Sports bar and microbrewery with hand-crafted ales, lagers, stouts and pilsners on tap. Upscale bar food like pan-roasted salmon, Boston clam chowder, stir-fries and burgers. Located near Fenway Park, so expect crowds when the Red Sox are playing. Brewery tours and tastings available.

✚ E7 ✉ 61 Brookline Avenue ☎ 617/536-2337 🚇 Kenmore

BOSTON CENTER FOR THE ARTS

www.bcaonline.org

Three stages at this South End performance space house several contemporary theater companies, including the provocative Company One and the cutting-edge SpeakEasy Stage Company.

✚ H7 ✉ 539 Tremont Street ☎ 617/426-5000 🚇 Back Bay Station

BOSTON PUBLIC LIBRARY

www.bpl.org

Regular free lunchtime concerts in summer.

✚ G7 ✉ Copley Square ☎ 617/536-5400 🚇 Copley

BUKOWSKI TAVERN

www.bukowskitavern.net

More than 100 varieties of beer are on offer at this friendly and unpretentious spot.

✚ F7 ✉ 50 Dalton Street ☎ 617/437-9999 🚇 Hynes Convention Center

BLUE LAWS

The legacy of the Puritans continues in strict state laws to curtail imbibing. Most bars in Boston and Cambridge close at 1am during the week, and 2am on the weekends—though you may find restaurants in Chinatown that still serve later. Happy-hour specials, such as 2-for-1 drinks, are also prohibited, though some bars serve free appetizers after work.

CASK 'N FLAGON

www.casknflagon.com

The perfect pit-stop before, during and after a Red Sox game, this rowdy sports bar has enough big-screen TVs to please the biggest fan.

✚ D7 ✉ 62 Brookline Avenue ☎ 617/536-4840 🚇 Kenmore

CITY BAR

www.citybarboston.com

Ultra-dim lighting and a stellar martini list make this cool intimate little gathering spot inside the Lenox Hotel perfect for a nightcap or a mysterious rendezvous.

✚ G6 ✉ 65 Exeter Street ☎ 617/933-4800 🚇 Copley, Back Bay Station

CLUB CAFÉ

www.clubcafe.com

A nightly playground for the gay and lesbian crowd, this upscale lounge, restaurant and "video bar" has something—and somebody—for everyone.

✚ H7 ✉ 209 Columbus Avenue ☎ 617/536-0966 🚇 Back Bay Station

DELUX CAFE

www.thedelux.com

Christmas lights, Elvis statues and Dr. Seuss wallpaper in the bathrooms. The interior here is as eclectic as its clientele. Try the tasty bar menu.

✚ H7 ✉ 100 Chandler Street ☎ 617/338-5258 🚇 Back Bay Station

FRANKLIN CAFÉ
franklincafe.com
Open very late, this busy restaurant is where chefs hang out after work. The home-cured corned beef and cabbage, and whole roast chicken, are legendary. Bar serving wines, cocktails and local microbrews. No reservations.
🔲 H8 ✉ 278 Shawmut Avenue ☎ 617/350-0010 🚇 Back Bay

HATCH SHELL
www.hatchshell.com
The Boston Pops Orchestra gives free concerts here in early July. The highlight is the concert with fireworks on July 4. Other musical groups perform throughout the summer.
🔲 H5 ✉ Esplanade, Embankment Road
☎ 617/626-4970 🚇 Charles/ MGH, Arlington

HOUSE OF BLUES BOSTON
www.houseofblues.com
Live blues, rhythm and blues, gospel, jazz and rockl. Also a private lounge, theater and restaurant.
🔲 E7 ✉ 15 Lansdowne Street ☎ 888/693-2583 🚇 Kenmore

HUNTINGTON THEATRE COMPANY
www.huntingtontheatre.org
Performances from Boston University's resident professional troupe include European and American, classical and

modern, comedies and musicals.
🔲 F7 ✉ 264 Huntington Avenue ☎ 617/266-0800 🚇 Symphony

JILLIAN'S
www.jilliansboston.com
Virtual sports, 200 high-tech games, 50 pool tables, plus five bars and bistro-style food.
🔲 E7 ✉ 145 Ipswich Street ☎ 617/437-0300 🕐 Daily 11am–2am 🚇 Kenmore

JORDAN HALL
www.necmusic.edu
This glittering and acoustically perfect venue, in the prestigious New England Conservatory, showcases the resident Boston Philharmonic, Boston Baroque and Cantata Singers. Conservatory students perform free concerts year-round.

🔲 E8 ✉ 30 Gainsborough Street, one block west of Symphony Hall ☎ 617/585-1260 🚇 Symphony

KINGS BOWL
www.kingsbowlamerica.com
This subterranean spot has the latest electronic scoring equipment. Relax in the hipster lounge after you tire of rolling strikes or gutter-balls.
🔲 F7 ✉ 50 Dalton Street ☎ 617/266-2695 🚇 Hynes Convention Center

MUSEUM OF FINE ARTS
www.mfa.org/film/
International, early and offbeat films.
🔲 E8 ✉ 465 Huntington Avenue ☎ 617/267-9300 🚇 Museum of Fine Arts

SYMPHONY HALL
www.bso.org
"Symphony" is home to the Boston Symphony Orchestra from September through May. The orchestra often performs on Friday afternoon, Saturday, Tuesday and Thursday evenings. Call for current schedule, as performance days vary from month-to-month. The Boston Pops Orchestra concerts are held here in December, May and June before moving to the Hatch Shell (▷ left) in July.
🔲 F7 ✉ 301 Massachusetts Avenue ☎ Box office 617/266-1200; general information 617/266-1492 🚇 Symphony

Restaurants

BRASSERIE JO (\$\$–\$\$\$)

www.brasseriejoboston.com
Opposite the Prudential Center, this traditional French brasserie specializes in Alsatian dishes, but serves all the French faves, from onion tart to coq au vin. Desserts are knockouts.

🗗 G7 ⊠ 120 Huntington Avenue ☎ 617/425-3240 🕐 Breakfast, lunch, dinner daily 🚇 Prudential

THE BUTCHER SHOP (\$\$\$)

thebutchershopboston.com
Meat, meat and more meat is king at this hip South End take on a European butcher/wine bar/restaurant. Choose from their own terrines, pâtés and sausages, great steaks and charcuterie.

🗗 H7 ⊠ 552 Tremont Street ☎ 617/423-4800 🕐 Mon–Fri 12–12, Sat 11am–midnight, Sun 11–11 🚇 Back Bay Station

CASA ROMERO (\$\$)

www.casaromero.com
Authentic, upscale Mexican dining. Generous portions of dishes including the signature tenderloin of pork marinated in oranges and smoked chipotle peppers.

🗗 F6 ⊠ 30 Gloucester Street ☎ 617/536-4341 🕐 Dinner daily 🚇 Hynes Convention Center

CLIO (\$\$\$)

www.cliorestaurant.com
Excellent fare that's creative without being weird. Good seafood preparations include chilled lobster and scallops with hot-and-sour bell-pepper broth. The sashimi bar is excellent.

🗗 F6 ⊠ Eliot Hotel, 370a Commonwealth Avenue, Back Bay ☎ 617/536-7200 🕐 Breakfast daily, dinner Tue–Sun 🚇 Hynes Convention Center

L'ESPALIER (\$\$\$)

www.lespalier.com
Superb contemporary fare with an emphasis on artisanal and New England ingredients in the formal setting of a 19th-century Back Bay house. Prix fixe.

🗗 F6 ⊠ 774 Boylston Street, Back Bay ☎ 617/262-3023 🕐 Lunch, dinner, tea daily 🚇 Hynes Convention Center

BAKERY CAFÉ

Flour Bakery (\$)
www.flourbakery.com
Grab melt-in-the-mouth breakfasts, lunches and dinners (plus delicious pies, cakes, pastries and cookies) at this neighborhood favorite.
🗗 H8 ⊠ 1595 Washington Street ☎ 617/267-4300 🚇 Back Bay/South End

HAMERSLEY'S BISTRO (\$\$\$)

www.hamersleysbistro.com
Excellent American-French dishes; try roast chicken with garlic and lemon.

🗗 H7 ⊠ 553 Tremont Street (at Clarendon), South End ☎ 617/423-2700 🕐 Dinner daily, brunch Sun 🚇 Back Bay Station

HARU (\$\$\$)

www.harusushi.com
This smart restaurant offers not just exemplary sushi, but tempura that melts in the mouth and a menu of favorites and inspired new creations.

🗗 G7 ⊠ 55 Huntington Avenue ☎ 617/536-0770 🕐 Lunch, dinner daily 🚇 Prudential

PETIT ROBERT BISTRO (\$\$)

www.petitrobertbistro.com
A bistro in the truest Parisian sense. Sit at the downstairs dessert bar to watch the pastry chef create your dessert.

🗗 E6 ⊠ 468 Commonwealth Avenue ☎ 617/375-0699 🕐 Lunch, dinner daily 🚇 Kenmore

UNION BAR & GRILLE (\$\$)

www.unionrestaurant.com
Stylish and often packed bar/restaurant, serving big plates of burgers and house-cured duck confit.

🗗 Off map at G9 ⊠ 1357 Washington Street ☎ 617/423-0555 🕐 Dinner daily, brunch Sat–Sun 🚇 Back Bay Station

This historic and multicultural city across the river from Boston is one of America's greatest academic centers, thanks to universities such as Harvard and the Massachusetts Institute of Technology.

Sights   **88–92**

Walk   **93**

Shopping   **94–95**

Entertainment
  and Nightlife **96–97**

Restaurants   **97–98**

Top 25   **TOP 25**

Harvard Square and
    Harvard University ▷ **88**
Harvard University and
    Art Museums ▷ **90**

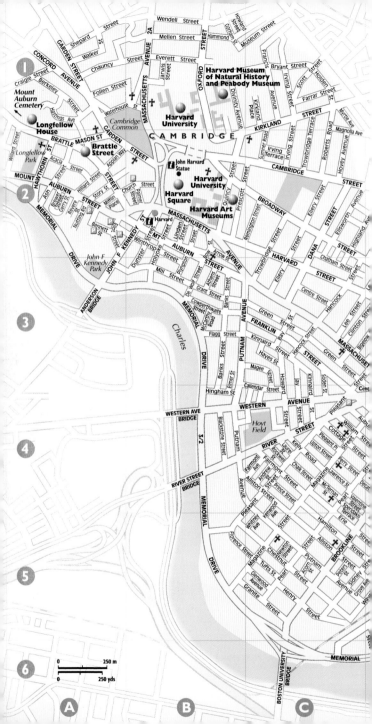

Harvard Square and Harvard University

TOP 25

PLAY THE CHESSMASTER $2 :200

- Harvard Yard
- Radcliffe Yard
- Browsing in a bookshop all evening

- Harvard is one place where a guided tour is essential. Stop in the Holyoke Arcade at 1350 Massachusetts Avenue to sign up for a free tour.
- Stroll down to the river to watch the rowing crews practice.

One of the most significant strands in the fabric of Bostonian life is the academic scene. In Cambridge you can walk through hallowed Harvard Yard in the footsteps of the great, then enjoy the funky scene in Harvard Square.

Harvard University Among the first things the Massachusetts Bay colonists did was provide for the training of ministers, and thus was founded, in 1636, one of the world's most respected seats of learning. Most of its historic buildings are in Harvard Yard, entered across the street from the First Parish Church. Ahead, in front of Bulfinch's University Hall, is a statue by Daniel Chester French of benefactor John Harvard.

The elegant 18th-century redbrick halls grouped around this, the Old Yard, are dormitories. Behind

Clockwise from left: A café in Harvard Square; students gather around the ornate gateway into a Harvard college; students on lawns outside Widener Memorial Library; a street musician entertains in Harvard Square; New Yard in the fall; pedestrians and students mingle in Harvard Square

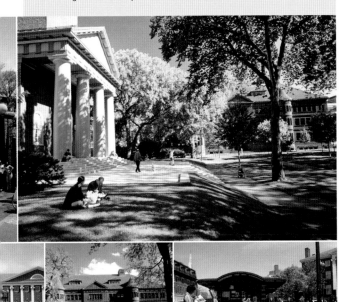

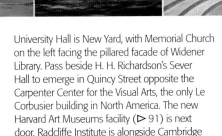

University Hall is New Yard, with Memorial Church on the left facing the pillared facade of Widener Library. Pass beside H. H. Richardson's Sever Hall to emerge in Quincy Street opposite the Carpenter Center for the Visual Arts, the only Le Corbusier building in North America. The new Harvard Art Museums facility (▷ 91) is next door. Radcliffe Institute is alongside Cambridge Common, around the lovely Radcliffe Yard.

Harvard Square The newsstand by the T is a famous landmark in this "square," which is actually more of a district. Here you can watch chess games, listen to street musicians, sit in an outdoor café, eat dessert at any time of day in Finale (30 Dunster Street), shop for trendy clothes, browse in bookshops or go to a club for jazz or reggae.

THE BASICS

www.harvard.edu

➕ B1/B2

✉ Harvard University: Harvard Yard, Peabody Street

☎ City of Cambridge Visitor Information Booth: 617/497-1630; University: 617/495-1573

🕐 Daily

🍴 Plenty nearby

Ⓣ Harvard

💷 Free

❓ Campus tours Mon–Fri hourly 9–3

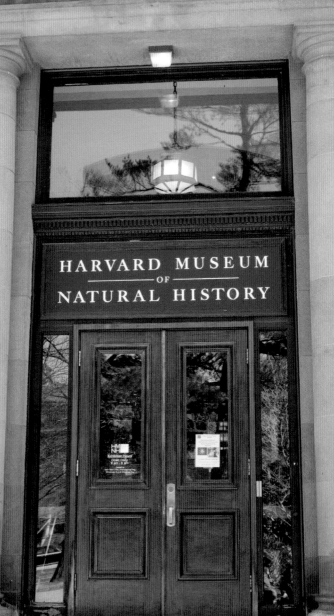

The facade of the
Museum of Natural
History (left); displays
(below and right)

TOP
25

Harvard University and Art Museums

Few universities have such an enviable, world-class collection of museums.

The Harvard Art Museums In 2014, the world-class Fogg, Busch-Reisinger, and Arthur M. Sackler museums re-opened under the umbrella title of the Harvard Art Museums. Uniting them all is a stunning glass roof, designed by Italian architect Renzo Piano. Within, the new galleries have distinctive spaces for their respective permanent collections. The Fogg is known for its comprehensive collection of Western European art (Italian early Renaissance, 17th-century Dutch, and 19th-century French and British paintings), the Busch-Reisinger for art from German-speaking countries (from Klee and Kandinsky to Anselm Kiefer and Gerhard Richter), while the Arthur M. Sackler's collections of Asian art, ancient Mediterranean and Byzantine works, Indian and Islamic art are world-renowned. With its new glass roof top, the renovated Calderwood Courtyard is a jaw-dropping example of modern architecture.

Harvard Museum of Natural History (HMNH) More than 3,000 models of 830 plant species are so realistic you cannot believe they are made of glass. Elsewhere are wild animals and birds, plus rocks and minerals, including precious gems.

Peabody Museum One of the world's finest collections recording human culture, especially strong in Native American peoples, is interpreted to provide historical and cultural backgrounds. The museum shop is a treasure trove.

THE BASICS

www.harvard.edu/
museums

🔲 B1/B2

✉ Harvard Art Museums: 32 Quincy Street. HMNH: 26 Oxford Street. Peabody: 11 Divinity Avenue

☎ Art museums: 617/495-9400. HMNH: 617/495-3045. Peabody: 617/496-1027

🕐 Art museums: Mon–Sat 10–5, Sun 1–5. HMNH and Peabody: daily 9–5

🚹 Very good

💰 Moderate. Art museums free Sat am. HMNH and Peabody free to Massachusetts residents Sep–May Wed pm, all year Sun am. CityPass applies

HIGHLIGHTS

● Impressionists (Fogg)
● Jade (Sackler)
● Glass flowers (HMNH)
● Native American exhibits (Peabody)

e to See

LONGFELLOW HOUSE AND BRATTLE STREET

www.nps.gov/long

In the pre-Revolutionary 1770s the land on either side of Brattle Street was owned by loyalist families, forced to quit when the Patriots took over the area in 1774. Henry Wadsworth Longfellow came to No. 105 Brattle Street as a lodger in 1837 and wrote many of his poems here. The historic gardens are open (free) year-round.

➕ A1/A2 ✉ 105 Brattle Street ☎ 617/876-4492 🕐 Late May–late Oct. Check for hours 🚇 Harvard, then pleasant walk (0.5 miles/0.8km) 💰 Inexpensive

MIT BUILDINGS

http://web.mit.edu

MIT has some impressive modern architecture. You are free to wander around the campus. Seek out Eero Saarinen's serene round chapel (1955). Don't miss Frank Gehry's latest whimsical Ray and Maria Stata Center for Computer, Information and Intelligence Sciences (2004), on Vassar Street. On and near Ames Street the low Wiesner and the tall Green buildings are the work of I. M. Pei (1964, 1985).

➕ E4 ✉ Massachusetts Avenue, Vassar Street, Ames Street 🚇 Kendall 💰 Free

MIT SCULPTURES

On the campus are two Henry Moore reclining figure pieces (1963, 1976), Alexander Calder's black steel *The Big Sail* (1965) and Michael Heizer's pink granite *Guennette* (1977).

➕ E5 ✉ Memorial Drive 🕐 Daily 🚇 Kendall 💰 Free

MOUNT AUBURN CEMETERY

A little out of the way, but a beautiful place. It was founded in 1831 as the country's first rural garden cemetery and is still very popular with bird and plant lovers. If it's a nice day you could walk here from Longfellow House (30 minutes). Longfellow now rests here, as does the artist Winslow Homer.

➕ Off map at A1 ✉ 580 Mount Auburn Street ☎ 617/547-7105 🕐 Daily 🚇 Harvard, then walk or Watertown bus

Mount Auburn Cemetery

Portrait of Henry Wadsworth Longfellow

Harvard Square

Cambridge, compact with noteworthy institutions, makes an excellent walk, dotted with history, entertainment and shops.

DISTANCE: 1 mile (1.6km) **ALLOW:** 3–4 hours

START

JOHN HARVARD STATUE, HARVARD YARD (▷ 88) ✚ B2 🚇 Harvard

END

CAMBRIDGE COMMON (▷ 89) ✚ B2 🚇 Harvard

❶ Begin on the Harvard University Green, on the site of the country's oldest college. Walk out of the gates and cross Massachusetts Avenue.

❷ Go straight down Church Street, passing numerous shops, until Church hits Brattle Street (▷ 92). Take a right on Brattle.

❸ Continue down Brattle Street, passing stately mansions, on the way to the Longfellow House (▷ 92), where Henry Wadsworth Longfellow once lived.

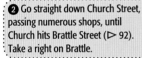

❹ Turn around on Brattle and head back toward Harvard Square, passing the American Repertory Theatre (▷ 96) on the way.

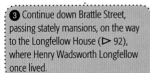

❽ Follow Massachusetts Avenue up to Cambridge Common, a magnet for students and professors looking to relax.

❼ Step into The Coop (▷ 94), Harvard's renowned bookstore. Turn right on Massachusetts Avenue for about one block, and turn right on Dunster Street to Finale with its fabulous desserts. Return to Massachusetts Avenue and turn left.

❻ Farther up, pass the Brattle Theatre (▷ 96), an independent cinema and one of the Square's most revered cultural stops. Follow Brattle to the left, where it meets up with Massachusetts Avenue.

❺ In the last blocks of Brattle, duck into the row's unique stores and gift shops.

93

Shopping

ABODEON

www.abodeon.com

A stockpile of modern and retro housewares. The vintage furniture is particularly impressive, though you may also want to pick up a few pieces of tableware (from local and global makers) while you're at it.

➕ Off map at B1 ✉ 1731 Massachusetts Avenue
☎ 617/497-0137 🚇 Harvard

BOSTON BEAD COMPANY

www.bostonbeadcompany.com

A little one-room shop filled with small bins of everything you need to make your own jewelry—ceramic beads, semi-precious stones, clasps, wire and more.

➕ B2 ✉ 23 Church Street
☎ 617/868-9777 🚇 Harvard

CAMBRIDGE ANTIQUE MARKET

www.marketantique.com

Another large Cambridge cooperative. Dealers sell china, glass, quilts, clothes, silver, jewelry and collectibles.

➕ Off map at G3 ✉ 201 Monsignor O'Brien Highway, diagonally opposite the Lechmere T ☎ 617/868-9655
🚇 Closed Mon 🚇 Lechmere

CAMBRIDGE ARTISTS' COOPERATIVE

www.cambridgeartistscoop.com

Quilts, weaving, jewelry, scarves—all made locally.

➕ B2 ✉ 59a Church Street
☎ 617/868-4434 🚇 Harvard

CARDULLO'S

www.cardullos.com

Crammed with international specialty foods, first-rate baked goods and the fixings for gift baskets, this family-run fixture is the place to pick up all your favorite foods and ingredients.

➕ A2 ✉ 6 Brattle Street
☎ 617/491-8888 🚇 Harvard

GROLIER POETRY BOOKSHOP

www.grolierpoetrybookshop.org

The US's only shop devoted entirely to poetry.

➕ B2 ✉ 6 Plympton Street ☎ 617/547-4648
🚇 Harvard

HARVARD BOOK STORE

www.harvard.com

Known for academic titles and other nonfiction. New and used books.

➕ B2 ✉ 1256 Massachusetts Avenue
☎ 617/661-1515
🚇 Harvard

BOOKSTORES

Cambridge, and Harvard Square in particular, has an amazing concentration of independent bookshops; just a handful are mentioned here. Pick up a complete guide from the information kiosk by Harvard Square T. Chainstores such as Barnes & Noble are to be found throughout Boston and Cambridge.

HARVARD COOP

thecoop.com

With its official Harvard logo clothing and gifts, the Coop is much more than a 130-year-old student store: four floors of books, dorm furnishing, fun café.

➕ B2 ✉ 1400 Massachusetts Avenue
☎ 617/499-2000
🚇 Harvard

HARVARD SQUARE

www.harvardsquare.com

Cambridge's Harvard Square is a maze of streets with bookshops, music shops and clothes stores, much of it geared for students. There's a wide variety of restaurants and cafés. Check out Brattle Street, Church Street, Eliot Street (with the Charles Square complex just off), JFK Street and Dunster Street. As some of the chains have moved into the area, so some of the smaller local shops have moved, or opened up, just north of Harvard and there's now a clutch of clothes and gift shops on Massachusetts Avenue.

HIDDEN SWEETS

www.hiddensweets.com

There's a lot more than candy inside, although you'll find the traditional "Boston Baked Beans" and maple sweets. Look here for lower prices on Harvard and Red Sox insignia items, and for smart-alec pins, bumper stickers and notepapers

that proclaim your progressive politics.
⊞ B2 ✉ 25 Brattle Street
☎ 617/497-2600 🚇 Harvard

JOIE DE VIVRE

www.joiedevivre.net
Selling toys for all ages, this fun store offers everything from wind-up toys and singing animals to kaleidoscopes, snowglobes and music boxes.
⊞ Off map at A1 ✉ 1792 Massachusetts Avenue
☎ 617/864-8188 🚇 Porter Square

LEAVITT & PEIRCE INC.

leavitt-peirce.com
A 130-year-old tobacco shop peddling bins of tobacco, pipes, men's shaving supplies and vintage chess sets.
⊞ B2 ✉ 1316 Massachusetts Avenue
☎ 617/547-0576 🚇 Harvard

LOOKS

www.looksclothing.com
Fun, up-to-date designs for the younger woman, with a changing selection of clothing, shoes, handcrafted local jewelry and accessories.
⊞ B2 ✉ 11–13 Holyoke Street ☎ 617/491-4251
🚇 Harvard

MINT JULEP

shopmintjulep.com
Attractive, stylish, but accessible and timeless clothing in luscious fabrics and colors are the style here. Accessories are equally well chosen, and the staff is helpful.

⊞ B2 ✉ 6 Church Street
☎ 617/576-6468 🚇 Harvard

NEWBURY COMICS

www.newburycomics.com
Music, especially rock & roll, sold as CDs, DVDs, LPs and singles. Look for pop culture merchandise, including comics, posters, T-shirts and much more.
⊞ B2 ✉ 36 JFK Street
☎ 617/491-0337 🚇 Harvard

NOMAD

nomadcambridge.com
Baskets handmade in Mexico, Asian masks, carved wooden switchplates from Brazil and jewelry and clothing from Europe—the global market makes its way to the shelves of Nomad.
⊞ Off map at B1 ✉ 1741 Massachusetts Avenue
☎ 617/497-6677 🚇 Porter

SCHOENHOF'S FOREIGN BOOKS

www.schoenhofs.com
For more than 150 years Schoenhof's has offered foreign-language books, including classics in original Greek or Latin, contemporary

literature, philosophy, children's books, poetry and language materials. French, German, Italian and Spanish titles are featured, with hundreds of other languages represented as well.
⊞ B2 ✉ 76A Mount Auburn Street ☎ 617/547-8855
🚇 Harvard

STELLABELLA TOYS

www.stellabellatoys.com
This shop wins awards for its selection of first-class, imaginative playthings.
⊞ C2 ✉ 1360 Cambridge Street ☎ 617/491-6290
🚇 Central

TESS & CARLOS

www.tessandcarlos.com
Stylish, classic clothes, shoes and accessories for men and women. The cashmere sweater collection and racks of apparel by Italian designers are particularly impressive.
⊞ A2 ✉ 20 Brattle Street
☎ 617/864-8377 🚇 Harvard

URBAN OUTFITTERS

www.urbanoutfitters.com
Where the young come to get that rugged look. Funky household goods.
⊞ B2 ✉ 11 JFK Street
☎ 617/864-0070 🚇 Harvard

THE WORLD'S ONLY CURIOUS GEORGE STORE

www.thecuriousgeorgestore.com
Devoted to the monkey that children love.
⊞ B2 ✉ 1 JFK Street
☎ 617/498-0062 🚇 Harvard

Entertainment and Nightlife

AMERICAN REPERTORY THEATRE
www.amrep.org
A highly regarded professional repertory company, staging classical and original drama.
⊞ A2 ✉ Loeb Drama Center, 64 Brattle Street
☎ 617/547-8300 🚇 Harvard

BRATTLE THEATRE
www.brattlefilm.org
Vintage films and film festivals attract fan to this small, one-screen theater.
⊞ A2 ✉ 40 Brattle Street
☎ 617/876-6837 🚇 Harvard

CANTAB LOUNGE
www.cantab-lounge.com
Neighborhood gathering spot, bar and grill, Cantab offers two venues with nightly performances of an eclectic variety of music and spoken word events. Monday night is Open Mike night.
⊞ C3 ✉ 738 Massachusetts Avenue ☎ 617/354-2685
🚇 Central

CLUB PASSIM
www.clubpassim.com
The Cambridge area's premier folk music venue attracts both up-and-coming and established performers.
⊞ B2 ✉ 47 Palmer Street
☎ 617/492-7679 🚇 Harvard

GREEN STREET
www.greenstreetgrill.com
Varied menu featuring seasonal entrées in a comfortable atmosphere. The cocktail menu is extensive, with fine wines and craft beers that make this neighborhood fixture a popular place to drink.
⊞ D4 ✉ 280 Green Street
☎ 617/876-1655 🕐 Dinner daily from 5.30pm 🚇 Central, then short walk

HARVARD FILM ARCHIVE
http://hcl.harvard.edu/hfa
Daily showings of cult and independent films at Harvard's Carpenter Center for the Visual Arts.
⊞ B2 ✉ 24 Quincy Street
☎ 617/495-4700 🚇 Harvard

HASTY PUDDING THEATER
www.hastypudding.org
Home to the touring Hasty Pudding Theatricals company and to the American Repertory Theatre's annual "New Stages" series of contemporary plays.

ALTERNATIVE DANCE
Contemporary and ethnic dance troupes perform at venues all over the city and beyond. In Boston, these include the **Boston Dance Alliance** (✉ 19 Clarendon Street ☎ 617/456-6295; www.bostondancealliance. org). In Cambridge, look for the **Multicultural Arts Center** (✉ 41 2nd Street ☎ 617/577-1400; www.cmacusa.org) and the **Dance Complex** (✉ 536 Massachusetts Avenue ☎ 617/547-9363; www. dancecomplex.org).

⊞ B2 ✉ 12 Holyoke Street
☎ 617/495-5205 🚇 Harvard

JOSÉ MATEO'S BALLET THEATRE
www.ballettheatre.org
Directed by José Mateo, this notable professional company performs a community-friendly mix of classical and contemporary ballet.
⊞ B2 ✉ 400 Harvard Street
☎ 617/354-7467 🚇 Harvard

THE MIDDLE EAST
www.mideastclub.com
The premier venue for alternative rock for not only Cambridge, but also Boston. The Middle East restaurant has three rooms for performers—upstairs, downstairs and in the restaurant.
⊞ C3 ✉ 472/480 Massachusetts Avenue
☎ 617/864-3278 🚇 Central

NOIR BAR
www.noir-bar.com
Sophisticated and sultry, this hip nook in the Charles Hotel provides comfortable couches for a late-night (2am) martini or seasonal cocktail seven days a week.
⊞ B2 ✉ 1 Bennett Street
☎ 617/661-8010 🚇 Harvard

REGATTABAR
www.regattabarjazz.com
First-class jazz acts come to Harvard Square at this classy bar in The Charles Hotel (▷ 112).
⊞ A2 ✉ 1 Bennett Street
☎ 617/661-5000 🕐 Closed Mon 🚇 Harvard

RYLES
www.rylesjazz.com
Another Cambridge hot spot, in Inman Square, with food downstairs. Emphasis is on Latin jazz. Weekly learn-to-salsa Latin dance night.
➕ E3 ✉ 212 Hampshire Street ☎ 617/876-9330 🕐 Music: Tue–Sun from 8.30pm, Sun jazz brunch: 10–3 🚇 Central then long walk or bus 83; Harvard then bus 69 along Cambridge Street

SANDERS THEATRE
www.fas.harvard.edu
A 1,600-seat neo-Gothic theater at Harvard, with classical and world music. Despite its size the 180-degree stage design allows an imtimate feel.

MOVIE TIME
The opening scenes of *The Social Network* movie were shot at The Thirsty Scholar pub. Order the Social Network Nachos and think of billionaire Mark Zuckerberg being dumped by Erika (Rooney Mara).
Thirsty Scholar ✉ 70 Beacon Street ☎ 617/497-2294; www.thirstyscholarpub.com 🚇 Harvard

---

➕ B2 ✉ Quincy Street at Cambridge Street
☎ 617/496-2222 🚇 Harvard

SCULLERS JAZZ CLUB
www.SkullersJazz.com
At the top of a Hilton hotel, this boasts a roll call of jazz greats over the years, from Diana Krall and Norah Jones to Michael Bublé and Jamie Cullum. Dinner and a show make a great night out.
➕ B4 ✉ 400 Soldiers Field Road ☎ 617/562-4111 🚇 Central

Restaurants

PRICES
Prices are approximate, based on a 3-course meal for one person.
\$\$\$	over \$40
\$\$	\$20–\$40
\$	under \$20

THE BLUE ROOM (\$\$\$)
www.theblueroom.net
This off-the-beaten-track restaurant is one of the best in Boston. The menu changes frequently, offers a creative wine list and features eclectic entrées such as tuna with star anise and ginger, plus a nightly vegetarian option.
➕ F3 ✉ 1 Kendall Square ☎ 617/494-9034 🕐 Dinner daily, brunch Sun 🚇 Kendall

BONDIR (\$\$\$)
www.bondircambridge.com
Rising star Jason Bond has a European passion for local produce, using classic techniques to create complex dishes with full flavors. Reservations essential.
➕ E3 ✉ 279A Broadway ☎ 617/661-0009 🕐 Wed–Mon 5pm–10pm, closed Tue 🚇 Central

BORDER CAFÉ (\$)
Fun, friendly and crowded, this popular restaurant serves large portions of tasty Cajun and Tex-Mex favorites, including fajitas, tacos, jambalaya and margaritas.
➕ B2 ✉ 32 Church Street ☎ 617/864-6100 🕐 Lunch, dinner daily (till late) 🚇 Harvard

CHRISTINA'S (\$)
www.christinasicecream.com
Christina's homemade ice cream and sorbet draw crowds. An ever-changing menu of flavors ranging from ordinary to unusual, such as burnt sugar, avocado, cardamom and bergamot.
➕ D2 ✉ 1255 Cambridge Street ☎ 617/492-7021 🕐 Daily 🚇 Harvard

CRAIGIE ON MAIN ($$$)

www.craigieonmain.com
The menu is so interesting and tempting that regulars opt for the "Chef's Whim" four- or six-course tasting menus offered on Sunday after 9pm. Dishes use only the freshest local ingredients.
➕ D4 ✉ 853 Main Street
☎ 617/497-5511 🕐 Dinner daily, brunch Sun 🚇 Central

HI-RISE ($)

This company is passionate about its bread, but also serves superb coffee, soups, sandwiches and preserves.
➕ B1 ✉ 1663 Massachusetts Avenue
☎ 617/492-3003 🕐 Mon–Fri 8–8, Sat–Sun 8–5 🚇 Harvard

L. A. BURDICK CHOCOLATE ($)

www.burdickchocolate.com
If heaven were a chocolate shop it might look something like this café.
➕ A2 ✉ 52 Brattle Street
☎ 617/491-4340 🕐 Daily
🚇 Harvard

LEGAL SEA FOODS ($$)

www.legalseafoods.com
Popular seafood chain serving good fish.
➕ F4 ✉ 5 Cambridge Center, Kendall Square
☎ 617/864-3400 🕐 Lunch, dinner daily 🚇 Kendall

MR. BARTLEY'S BURGER COTTAGE ($)

Choose from more than two dozen burgers with sweet potato fries, plus salads, sandwiches and desserts.
➕ B2 ✉ 1246 Massachusetts Avenue
☎ 617/354-6559 🕐 Lunch, dinner Mon–Sat. Closed Sun
🚇 Harvard

OLEANA ($$–$$$)

www.oleanarestaurant.com
Thanks to her innovative cuisine, based on eastern Mediterranean tradition, owner Ana Sortun is on most critics' lists of New England's leading chefs. Using her husband's locally grown organic vegetables, Sortun creates light, healthy and delicately spiced dishes that win rave reviews.
➕ E3 ✉ 134 Hampshire Street ☎ 617/661-0505
🕐 Dinner nightly from 5.30
🚇 Central

PARK ($$)

parkcambridge.com
With its armchairs and sofas, this neighborhood favorite serves a tempting mix of contemporary European and American dishes late into the night. Lively bar.

BRUNCH

Henrietta's Table ($$–$$$)
The Charles Hotel (▷ 112). Honest to goodness New England cooking.
➕ B2 ✉ 1 Bennett Street ☎ 617/661-5005
🕐 Breakfast daily, lunch Mon–Fri, brunch, supper Sat–Sun 🚇 Harvard

---

➕ B2 ✉ 59 JFK Street
☎ 617/491-9851 🕐 Mon–Wed 5pm–1am, Thu–Sat 5pm–2am, Sun 10am–1am
🚇 Harvard

RIALTO ($$$)

www.rialto-restaurant.com
Star chef Jody Adams whips up a superb Mediterranean menu made from local ingredients and produce. More casual, but equally delicious, food is served in the restaurant's bar area.
➕ A2 ✉ The Charles Hotel, 1 Bennett Street ☎ 617/661-5050 🕐 Dinner daily
🚇 Harvard

SANDRINE'S ($$$)

www.sandrines.com
Relaxed dining on Alsatian dishes. Don't skip the salads (perhaps Cortland apples, blue cheese and spiced cashews) en route to the silky scallops or a choucroute garnie of meats and sausages cooked in Riesling.
➕ A2 ✉ 8 Holyoke Street
☎ 617/497-5300 🕐 Lunch Mon–Sat, dinner daily
🚇 Harvard

TORY ROW ($$)

www.toryrow.us
A meeting place for residents and Harvard students, bikers and visitors, this lively watering hole offers a wide range of dishes, from salads and sandwiches to grilled fish and steaks.
➕ B2 ✉ 3 Brattle Street
☎ 617/876-8769 🕐 Daily 9am–11pm 🚇 Harvard

You could easily spend weeks in Boston and not come to the end of all the city has to offer. Dozens of historical and cultural attractions lie within easy day-trip reach and are worth exploring in their own right.

Sights	102–104	Top 25	**TOP 25**
Excursions	105–106	Boston Harbor Islands ▷ **102**	
		JFK Library and Museum ▷ **103**	

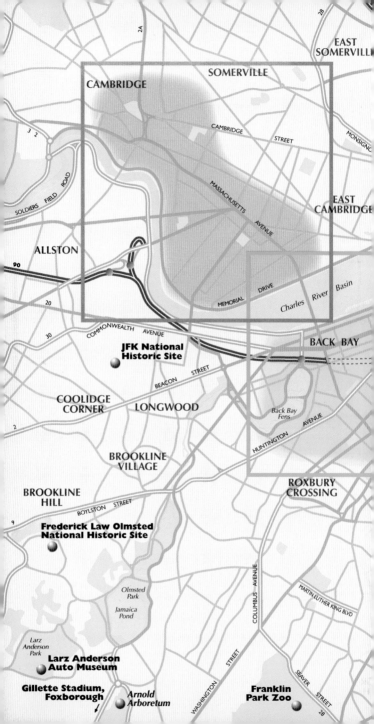

EAST
SOMERVILLE

28

2A

SOMERVILLE

CAMBRIDGE

CAMBRIDGE STREET

MONSIGNC

3 2

MASSACHUSETTS

SOLDIERS FIELD ROAD

AVENUE

EAST
CAMBRIDGE

ALLSTON

DRIVE

Charles River Basin

90

MEMORIAL

20

30

COMMONWEALTH AVENUE

JFK National
Historic Site

BACK BAY

BEACON STREET

COOLIDGE
CORNER

LONGWOOD

Back Bay
Fens

AVENUE

2

HUNTINGTON

BROOKLINE
VILLAGE

ROXBURY
CROSSING

BROOKLINE
HILL

9

BOYLSTON STREET

Frederick Law Olmsted
National Historic Site

COLUMBUS AVENUE

MARTIN LUTHER KING BLVD

Olmsted
Park

Jamaica
Pond

Larz
Anderson
Park

Larz Anderson
Auto Museum

WASHINGTON STREET

Gillette Stadium,
Foxborough

Arnold
Arboretum

Franklin
Park Zoo

SEAVER STREET

28

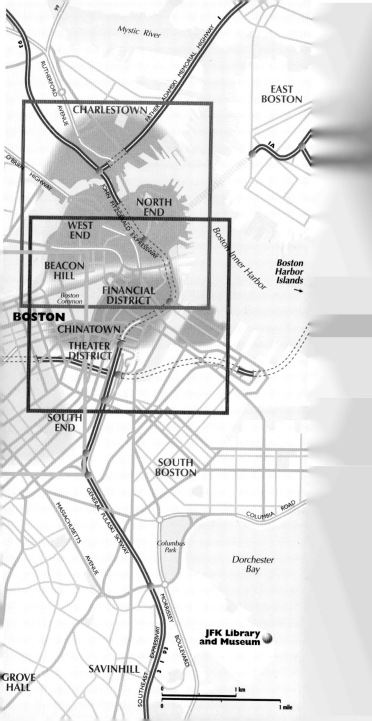

Boston Harbor Islands

Peddocks Island in Boston Harbor

THE BASICS

www.bostonharborislands.org

www.nps.gov/boha/index.htm

🚩 Off map at M5

✉ Boston Harbor Islands Visitor Pavilion, 191 Atlantic Avenue

☎ 617/223-8666

🕐 Georges Island: May to mid-Oct daily ferries. The other islands: May–Labor Day daily

🍴 Snack bar and barbecues on Georges. No drinking water on any islands. Take a picnic

🚢 Long Wharf, Quincy Shipyard and Logan Airport to Georges Island. Long Wharf and Quincy Shipyard to other islands. From Jun 1–Labor Day free water shuttles between islands

♿ Poor

💰 Ferry expensive. Water taxi free

❓ Organized activities and tours including lighthouse and occasional winter trips. Check websites for details

HIGHLIGHTS

● The sense of escape
● Picnicking on a beach
● Fort Warren's dungeons
● Views of Boston's skyline
● Bird-watching on all the islands

Gather wild raspberries, picnic on a beach, visit a ruined fort—all within sight of the city? These wildernesses are ringed by Boston, its airport and suburbs: It's just incredible they've escaped development.

National Recreation Area Once defensive sites and home to prisons and poorhouses, the Boston Harbor Islands were largely ignored until they became a National Recreation Area in 1996. People are beginning to appreciate these havens of wildlife, so near yet so distant in feel.

Island hopping It's a 45-minute ferry ride from Long Wharf to Georges Island. From here water taxis loop to Lovells, Peddocks, Bumpkin and Grape. The islands are small, so you can visit more than one in a day; each has its own character. Georges attracts most visitors. All have picnic areas (there's no fresh water). Take guided walks, hike trails on your own or just beachcomb (beaches are mostly pebbly). Lovells has a sandy, supervised swimming beach.

Something for everyone On Georges clamber over Fort Warren (find the hidden spiral staircase and get superb views of the city). Peddocks and Lovells also have ruined forts. Bumpkin is where to pick raspberries. Join the hares on Lovells; study the wildlife in the rock pools, salt marsh and woodland on Peddocks; and on Grape, crunch along beaches covered in iridescent blue mussel shells.

"A man may die, nations may rise and fall, but an idea lives on," said the late president John F. Kennedy, whose life, leadership and legacy are brilliantly evoked in this dramatic museum by the sea.

The setting The presidential library and its museum, constructed in 1979, are housed in an I. M. Pei building on Dorchester Bay, 4 miles (6.5km) southeast of downtown Boston. The building's two towers, of dark glass and smooth white concrete, command fine views of the city, the bay and Boston Harbor Islands. The lawns, dune grass and wild roses on the grounds recall the Kennedy summer home on Cape Cod.

The Museum An introductory film covers Kennedy's early years, from his childhood to the 1960 presidential campaign. Re-created settings include the White House corridors and the Oval Office, complete with the coconut inscribed "HELP" that led to his rescue after his naval ship sank in the Pacific. Videos cover significant events such as the Cuban Missile Crisis, space exploration and the assassination. Family photographs and exhibits cover the life and work of Jacqueline Kennedy Onassis.

The Presidential Library This is one of 13 presidential libraries holding the papers of 13 of the US presidents since Herbert Hoover. The Presidential Library System allows presidents to establish a library and museum.

THE BASICS

www.jfklibrary.org
🔲 Off map at J9
✉ Columbia Point, Dorchester (Route 3/I-93 exit 15)
☎ 617/514-1600
🕐 Daily 9–5
🍴 Café on premises
🚇 JFK/U Mass then free shuttle bus
♿ Excellent
💲 Moderate
❓ Shop

HIGHLIGHTS

● The building, its setting and views
● Introductory video
● Oval Office
● Film and sound clips

TIP

● At the JFK Library, don't miss the Hemingway collection, which includes manuscripts and artifacts from the late, great writer.

FARTHER AFIELD TOP 25

More to See

ARNOLD ARBORETUM
www.arboretum.harvard.edu
Stunning in all seasons, this hilly park is part of the "Emerald Necklace."
➕ Off map at B9 ✉ 125 Arborway, Jamaica Plain ☎ 617/524-1718 ◷ Daily dawn–dusk 🚇 Orange line to Forest Hills 💷 Free

FRANKLIN PARK ZOO
www.zoonewengland.org
Wander through an African tropical forest, stroke small animals at the Children's Zoo and visit the lions.
➕ Off map at G9 ✉ 1 Franklin Park Road ☎ 617/541-5466 ◷ Daily 🍴 Café or picnic 🚇 Forest Hills, then bus 16 💷 Moderate

FREDERICK LAW OLMSTED NATIONAL HISTORIC SITE
www.nps.gov/frla
This famous landscape architect designed Boston Common. Here you can tour the grounds and arrange weekend walking tours.
➕ Off map at A9 ✉ 99 Warren Street ☎ 617/566-1689 ◷ Daily 🚇 Brookline Hills (Green line D) then 0.75-mile (1.2km) walk 💷 Free

GILLETTE STADIUM
www.gillettestadium.com
Gillette Stadium is home to the New England Patriots (Aug–Dec) and men's pro soccer team, New England Revolution (Mar–Oct).
➕ Off map at B9 ✉ Route 1, Foxborough ☎ 800/543-1776. Ticketmaster: 617/931-2000

JFK NATIONAL HISTORIC SITE
Take a trip to Brookline and President Kennedy's boyhood home, filled with photographs and other memorabilia.
➕ A7 ✉ 83 Beals Street ☎ 617/566-7937 ◷ May–Oct Wed–Sun 9.30–5 🚇 Coolidge Corner (Green line C) 💷 Tour inexpensive

LARZ ANDERSON AUTO MUSEUM
www.larzanderson.org
America's oldest private automobile collection—highlights include antique Mercedes and French cars.
➕ Off map at B9 ✉ 15 Newton Street, Brookline ☎ 617/522-6547 ◷ Tue–Sun 10–4 🚇 Reservoir (Green line D), bus 51 💷 Inexpensive

Blazing fall color at the Arnold Arboretum

Excursions

PLYMOUTH

The Pilgrims left Plymouth, England, for the New World on the *Mayflower*. Their landing of 1620 (the exact location is debated) is commemorated on the waterfront by Plymouth Rock, the town having been named after the Devon port from where they set sail. Don't expect a boulder, however; most visitors are disappointed by the small size of the granite stone.

A more satisfying way to get in touch with the history of Massachusetts' first settlers is to visit them at Plimoth Plantation, a meticulously researched reproduction Pilgrim settlement 3 miles (5km) south. Here interpreters in period costume chat with visitors while getting on with their chores. The excellent curators work hard to make the village site accessible and display exhibits including how the Pilgrims' diet related to the seasons. At another exhibit, the Wampanoag Homesite, the Native Americans on whose ancestors' land the Pilgrims settled tell of their experiences. Also affiliated with the museum is the *Mayflower II,* a seaworthy replica of the ship that the Pilgrims sailed from England to the New World. Costumed interpreters provide below-decks tours and insight into the perilous crossing.

Plymouth is a popular destination and offers motels, restaurants and other attractions catering to visitors—some of them authentic, others tacky. One worth a stop is the Pilgrim Hall Museum, which is full of impressive artifacts once owned by the Pilgrims, including furniture, clothing and armor. A reproduction of the 1636 Plimoth Grist Mill operates twice a week, using water power to mill organic corn, which is for sale. One of the best times to visit Plymouth is during Thanksgiving, when the town pulls out all the stops with a parade and other events—and modern-day Native Americans stage an annual protest they call the "National Day of Mourning."

THE BASICS

www.seeplymouth.com
Distance: 50 miles (80km)
Journey Time: 1 hour
☎ Plimoth Plantation: 508/746-1622
◉ Plimoth Plantation and *Mayflower II:* late Mar–Nov
🚃 From South Station
♿ Plimoth Plantation, *Mayflower II:* expensive. Pilgrim Hall Museum: moderate
ℹ Destination Plymouth
✉ 134 Court Street
☎ 508/747-7533

HIGHLIGHTS

● Plimoth Plantation
● The Wampanoag Homesite
● The *Mayflower II*
● Plymouth Rock
● Pilgrim Hall Museum

THE BASICS

Concord/Lexington
www.nps.gov/mima
Distance: 20 miles (32km)
Journey Time: 40 minutes
🕐 Daily ranger tours explain the events of 1775 (May–Oct)
🚉 From North Station
🛈 Minute Man Visitor Center
✉ 250 North Great Road, Lincoln
☎ 978/369-6993

THE BASICS

Salem
www.salem.org
Distance: 16 miles (26km)
Journey Time: 30 minutes
🕐 Peabody Essex Museum: Tue–Sun, hol Mon 10–5. Witch Museum: daily
🚉 From North Station
🚢 From Long Wharf
💷 Peabody Essex Museum: expensive. Witch Museum: moderate
🛈 Destination Salem
✉ 63 Wharf Street
☎ 978/744-3663

From left: Captain Parker statue in Lexington; bandstand; Roger Conant statue; House of the Seven Gables in Salem; Witch Museum sign

LEXINGTON AND CONCORD

These lovely towns are immortalized by events that sparked the first shots of the Revolution.

It was to Lexington, where Patriot leaders were staying, that Paul Revere made his famous ride to warn of British plans to seize a cache of arms in Concord. It was on Concord's North Bridge, on April 19, 1775, that the "shot heard round the world" was fired. Concord has a literary past, too, as the home of influential early 19th-century writers and thinkers Henry David Thoreau, Ralph Waldo Emerson, Nathaniel Hawthorne and Louisa May Alcott. Visit their houses, and their graves in Sleepy Hollow Cemetery.

SALEM

To many, Salem means witches, so it's not surprising to find a range of interpretations of the mass hysteria that hit the town in the 1690s.

The most popular attraction is the Salem Witch Museum, which treads a fine line between cheap thrills and historical accuracy in telling the macabre tale of the trials that claimed 19 lives. Other sites worth visiting are the Witch House, which belonged to the presiding judge, and the affecting memorial to the victims on Salem Common.

Less well known but far more striking once you're there is that the town also has a rich maritime history and some of the best Federal architecture in America. In the 18th and early 19th centuries Salem's prosperous shipbuilders, merchants and sea captains built graceful houses and filled them with beautiful things. Many of these objects are in the Peabody Essex Museum.

The places to rest your head around Boston run from family-run bed-and-breakfasts to elaborate, world-class hotels. The majority are a convenient walking distance from the major sights.

Introduction   108

Budget Hotels   109

Mid-Range Hotels   110–111

Luxury Hotels   112

Introduction

Boston has no shortage of places to stay, all to suit your personal preferences for style, noise level, amenities and location.

Bed-and-Breakfasts and Inns

Bed-and-breakfasts are often run out of a private home. They normally include a modest bedroom, plus a home-cooked breakfast, at a reasonable price. Boston and Cambridge have a number of such establishments in the city. A bit more luxurious and larger than a bed-and-breakfast, the best inns around Boston are often housed in historic buildings or town houses. They also often include breakfast, though sometimes charge a separate fee. Some have such modern amenities as flat-screen televisions, CD players and whirlpool tubs.

Boutique and Luxury Hotels

Over the last several years, a stable of chic, modern small hotels has cropped up. The majority offer stylish, contemporary design, hip restaurants on the property and concierge services. They are mostly in and around downtown Boston. Scattered throughout Boston's most popular neighborhoods (from Back Bay and Downtown to Harvard Square), the area's luxury hotels cater to the traveler's every need and whim. Some offer quirky amenities (authors library in the lobby at Harvard Square's Charles Hotel) alongside services such as in-room massages and personal shoppers.

HISTORIC HOTELS

A handful of the city's most history-laden sites are also places you can stay the night. **The Omni Parker House** (▷ 111) is America's longest continuously operating luxury hotel. Opened in 1855, it was the meeting site of a literary group that included Ralph Waldo Emerson and Nathaniel Hawthorne. Later, its dining room gained a place in Boston history as the site of President (then Senator) John F. Kennedy's proposal to Jacqueline Bouvier. The **Fairmont Copley Plaza** (▷ 112) has witnessed many of Boston's grandest celebrations.

Budget Hotels

PRICES

Expect to pay between $75 and $150 per night for a budget hotel.

40 BERKELEY
www.40berkeley.com
Located in Boston's South End, this affordable hostel offers single, double and dorm-style rooms with shared bathrooms for reasonable prices. Full breakfast is included, and there is a TV room.
✚ H7 ✉ 40 Berkeley Street ☎ 617/375-2524 🚇 Back Bay Station

CHANDLER INN
www.chandlerinn.com
Basic 56-room hotel in the attractive South End. Gay-friendly. Short walk to Tremont Street restaurant row and Copley Square.

OUT OF TOWN
To reduce hotel costs, consider staying in Concord, Salem or Rockport, all 40–60 minutes from Boston and served by regular train services. Contact:
Concord Chamber of Commerce
☎ 978/369-3120; www.concordchamberof commerce.org
Destination Salem
☎ 978/744-3663; www. salem.org
Rockport Chamber of Commerce ☎ 978/283-1601; www.rockportusa.com

✚ H7 ✉ 26 Chandler Street ☎ 617/482-3450 or 800/ 842-3450; fax 617/542-3428 🚇 Back Bay Station

COLLEGE CLUB
www.thecollegeclubofboston. com
You don't have to be a student to book a room here. Some rooms have shared bathrooms.
✚ G6 ✉ 44 Commonwealth Avenue ☎ 617/536-9510; fax 617/247-8537 🚇 Arlington

COMFORT INN
www.comfortinn.com
Three miles (5km) south of town. Outdoor pool. 133 rooms.
✚ Off map at K9 ✉ 900 Morrissey Boulevard, Dorchester ☎ 617/287-9200; fax 617/282-2365 🚇 JFK/U Mass, then half-hourly hotel shuttle bus 7am–10pm

HI-BOSTON
www.hiusa.org/boston/
This purpose-built hostel close to Chinatown offers great value in 3-, 4- or 6-bedded rooms. Use the café or the kitchen; join in daily programs, lectures, films and workshops.
✚ J6 ✉ 19 Stuart Street ☎ 617/536-9455 🚇 Boylston, Chinatown

THE INN AT LONG-WOOD MEDICAL
www.innatlongwood.com
Located less than a mile from Fenway Park and the Museum of Fine Arts.
✚ D9 ✉ 342 Longwood Avenue ☎ 617/731-4700 or 800/468-2378; fax 617/731-

4870 🚇 Green line D to Longwood

JOHN JEFFRIES HOUSE
www.johnjeffrieshouse.com
Four-floor brick inn on Beacon Hill; 46 tiny rooms. The two-room suites are better value.
✚ H5 ✉ 14 David Mugar Way (formerly Embankment Road) at Charles Circle ☎ 617/367-1866; fax 617/ 742-0313 🚇 Charles/MGH

NEWBURY GUEST HOUSE
www.newburyguesthouse.com
Victorian-style rooms—32 in all—in three connected redbrick row houses. Excellent value, popular; reserve well ahead.
✚ G6 ✉ 261 Newbury Street, Back Bay ☎ 617/ 670-6000 or 800/437-7668; fax 617/670-6100 🚇 Copley, Hynes Convention Center

BED-AND-BREAKFAST
Double occupancy in bed-and-breakfast accommodation ranges from $90 to $180. Try the **Bed-and-Breakfast Agency of Boston**, a helpful, friendly agency that will find you accommodation in historic houses and restored waterfront lofts. Nightly, weekly, monthly and winter rates (✉ 47 Commercial Wharf ☎ 617/ 720-3540, 800/248-9262 or 0800 895 128 from the UK; fax 617/523-5761; www. boston-bnagency.com).

Mid-Range Hotels

PRICES

Expect to pay between $150 and $275 per night for a mid-range hotel.

AMES BOSTON HOTEL

www.ameshotel.com
The Ames Building is now a smart, luxury boutique hotel with 114 rooms. The minimalist but luxurious interior contrasts with the 19th-century exterior. Smart fitness center; Continental breakfast.
✚ K5 ✉ 1 Court Street ☎ 617/979-8100 🚇 Government Center

BEACON HILL HOTEL AND BISTRO

www.beaconhillhotel.com
Thirteen tasteful rooms in two linked townhouses. Lovely roof deck.
✚ H5 ✉ 25 Charles Street ☎ 617/723-7575 or 888/959-2442; fax 617/723-7525 🚇 Charles/MGH

BOSTON PARK PLAZA

www.bostonparkplaza.com
Elegant hotel built in 1927, with 1,053 rooms. Near the Public Garden and Theater District. Family friendly.
✚ H6 ✉ 64 Arlington Street ☎ 617/426-2000 or 800/225-2008; fax 617/426-5545 🚇 Arlington

LA CAPELLA SUITES

www.lacappellasuites.com
Bare-bones B&B accommodations in the North End give you enviable access to the restaurants and cafés of Hanover Street.
✚ K4 ✉ 290 North Street ☎ 617/523-9020 🚇 Haymarket

COLONNADE

www.colonnadehotel.com
Behind the bland 1960s facade of this 285-room hotel near the Pru are newly decorated rooms. Rooftop pool. Home of Brasserie JO.
✚ F7 ✉ 120 Huntington Avenue, Back Bay ☎ 617/424-7000 or 800/962-3030; fax 617/424-1717 🚇 Prudential

CONSTITUTION INN

www.constitutioninn.org
Within sight of its namesake ship, this spartan, nautically themed inn offers military discounts.

MORE OPTIONS

Hyatt Regency, Cambridge
www.cambridge.hyatt.com
On the Charles River, with a revolving rooftop lounge. 469 rooms.
✉ 575 Memorial Drive ☎ 617/492-1234 or 800/233-1234; fax 617/491-6906 🚇 Kendall

A Cambridge House
www.acambridgehouse.com
A Victorian bed-and-breakfast inn in north Cambridge. 15 rooms.
✉ 2218 Massachusetts Avenue ☎ 617/491-6300 or 800/232-9989; fax 617/868-2848 🚇 Davis, Porter

✚ K2 ✉ 150 3rd Avenue, Charlestown ☎ 617/241-8400 🚇 North Station

COURTYARD BOSTON DOWNTOWN

www.marriott.com
In the heart of the Theatre District, in an historic 1925 building.
✚ J6 ✉ 275 Tremont Street ☎ 617/426-1400; fax 617/482-6730 🚇 Boylston

ELIOT

www.eliothotel.com
Elegance, comfort and value. 95 rooms and suites with living room and kitchenette.
✚ E6 ✉ 370 Commonwealth Avenue, Back Bay ☎ 617/267-1607 or 800/44 ELIOT; fax 617/536-9114 🚇 Hynes Convention Center

GRYPHON HOUSE

www.innboston.com
Each of the eight rooms at this well-appointed B&B has its own distinct identity.
✚ E6 ✉ 9 Bay State Road ☎ 617/375-9003 🚇 Kenmore

HAMPTON INN & SUITES BOSTON CROSSTOWN CENTER

www.bostonhamptoninn.com
Good value at this modern-feeling hotel on the edge of the South End. Free shuttle to many city attractions.
✚ F7 ✉ 811 Massachusetts Avenue ☎ 617/445-6400 🚇 Massachusetts Avenue (Orange line)

HARBORSIDE INN
www.harborsideinnboston.com
A downtown location and elegant furnishings make this hotel good value for the money.
🏨 K5 ✉ 185 State Street ☎ 617/723-7500; fax 617/670-6015 🚇 State

HILTON BOSTON BACK BAY
www.hilton.com
Convenient to the Pru and Hynes centers. 390 rooms.
🏨 F7 ✉ 40 Dalton Street, Back Bay ☎ 617/236-1100 or 800/874-0663; fax 617/867-6104 🚇 Prudential, Hynes Convention Center

HOTEL MARLOWE
www.hotelmarlowe.com
This elegant hotel is big and boutique. Rooms are lushly decorated and the service is excellent.
🏨 H3 ✉ 24 Edwin Land Boulevard ☎ 617/868-8000 or 800/825-7140 🚇 Lechmere

HOTEL VERITAS
thehotelveritas.com
This independently owned, 31-room hotel is ideal for exploring Cambridge, yet is within easy reach of downtown Boston.
🏨 B2 ✉ 1 Remington Street, Cambridge ☎ 617/515-3390 🚇 Harvard

HYATT REGENCY BOSTON
www.regencyboston.hyatt.com
Family- and pet-friendly, this 22-floor, 500-room hotel is close to Faneuil Hall and the Theater District.
🏨 J6 ✉ One Avenue de Lafayette ☎ 617/912-1234 or 800/492-8804; fax 617/451-2198 🚇 Downtown Crossing

JEWEL OF NEWBURY
www.jewelboston.com
Take an exotic vacation-within-a-vacation with the eye-popping array of antiques from around the world at this intimate Back Bay B&B. Close to Copley Sqaure and Boston Common.
🏨 F7 ✉ 254 Newbury Street ☎ 617/536-5523 🚇 Hynes Convention Center

KENDALL HOTEL
kendallhotel.com
A former firehouse close to MIT and just over the bridge to Boston has been converted into a comfortable boutique hotel, complete with Americana furnishings.
🏨 F4 ✉ 350 Main Street, Cambridge ☎ 866/566-1300 🚇 Kendall

MARY PRENTISS INN
maryprentissinn.com
A 20-room, antiques-filled bed-and-breakfast in an 1843 mansion with modern amenities.
🏨 E9 ✉ 6 Prentiss Street ☎ 617/661-2929; fax 617/661-5989 🚇 Porter

OMNI PARKER HOUSE
www.omnihotels.com
A rather staid 551-room, 19th-century hotel, near Boston Common. The Parker House roll and Boston cream pie were invented here.
🏨 J5 ✉ 60 School Street, Downtown ☎ 617/227-8600 or 800/843-6664; fax 617/742-5729 🚇 Park Street

SHERATON BOSTON
www.starwood.com/sheraton
1,215 rooms in two 29-floor towers, connected by interior walkways to the Pru and Hynes. Caters to business travelers, but is also family-friendly.
🏨 G7 ✉ Prudential Center, 39 Dalton Street ☎ 617/236-2000 or 888/627-7054; fax 617/236-1702 🚇 Prudential, Hynes Convention Center

WHERE TO STAY MID-RANGE HOTELS

Luxury Hotels

PRICES

Expect to pay more than $275 per night for a luxury hotel.

BOSTON HARBOR

www.bhh.com
Modern, elegant, 230-room hotel on the waterfront. It's worth paying a little more for harbor views. Good restaurant, with views.
L5 ⊠ 70 Rowes Wharf
☎ 617/439-7000 or 800/752-7077; fax 617/330-9450
Ⓠ Aquarium

THE CHARLES HOTEL

www.charleshotel.com
Modern 295-room, 46-suite hotel in Harvard Square. Home to Henrietta's Table (panel, ▷ 98) and Regattabar (▷ 96).
B2 ⊠ 1 Bennett Street, Cambridge ☎ 617/864-1200 or 800/882-1818; fax 617/864-5715 Ⓠ Harvard

COPLEY SQUARE

www.copleysquarehotel.com
143-room hotel with European flavor. Fitness facility, XHALE restaurant.
G6 ⊠ 47 Huntington Avenue, Back Bay ☎ 617/536-9000 or 800/225-7062; fax 617/421-1402 Ⓠ Copley

FAIRMONT COPLEY PLAZA

www.fairmont.com
A "grand dame" of Boston, with sumptuous decor. 383 rooms.
G6 ⊠ 138 St. James Avenue, Back Bay ☎ 617/267-5300 or 866/540-4417; fax 617/267-7668 Ⓠ Copley

FOUR SEASONS

www.fourseasons.com/boston
Top-notch elegance and service. Fine dining in the Bristol Lounge (▷ 61). 272 rooms.
H6 ⊠ 200 Boylston Street, Back Bay ☎ 617/338-4400 or 800/332-3442; fax 617/423-0154 Ⓠ Arlington

LANGHAM HOTEL

www.langhamhotels.com
Historic 1920s building with luxurious comforts. 326 rooms. Café Fleuri restaurant (▷ 61).
K5 ⊠ 250 Franklin Street ☎ 617/451-1900; fax 617/423-2844 Ⓠ State, Downtown Crossing

LENOX

www.lenoxhotel.com
This 212-room independent is one of the best.
G6 ⊠ 710 Boylston Street ☎ 617/536-5300 or 800/225-7676; fax 617/267-1237 Ⓠ Copley

THE LIBERTY HOTEL

www.libertyhotel.com
Brilliant transformation of a grim old city jail into a stunning contemporary

W HOTEL BOSTON

Dramatic, contemporary and sophisticated. Rooms are high-tech, chic and modern with 235 rooms on 28 floors.
J6 ⊠ 100 Stuart Street ☎ 617/261-8700; fax 617/261-8725 Ⓠ Boylston

hotel with river views. There's just enough tongue-in-cheek reference to its past to be fun.
H4 ⊠ 215 Charles Street ☎ 617/224-4000 or 866/507-5245 Ⓠ Charles/MGH

MILLENNIUM BOSTONIAN

www.millenniumhotels.com
This 201-room hotel is more intimate than some, and offers comfort without glitz. North 26 Restaurant.
K5 ⊠ Faneuil Hall Marketplace ☎ 617/523-3600 or 866/866-8086; fax 617/523–2454 Ⓠ State, Government Center

NINE ZERO

www.ninezero.com
When the stars are in town, they stay at this chic boutique hotel on the Freedom Trail. Rooms have all the latest gadgets and amenities.
J6 ⊠ 90 Tremont Street ☎ 617/772-5800; fax 617/772-5810 Ⓠ Park Street

SEAPORT HOTEL

www.seaportboston.com
In Boston's newest downtown neighborhood, the hotel is opposite the World Trade Center and the new Institute of Contemporary Art. It's a class act, with fine dining at Aura (▷ 61), a full spa, in-room wireless and interactive web portal.
M6 ⊠ 1 Seaport Lane (Northern Avenue) ☎ 617/385-4000 or 800/440-3318 Ⓠ World Trade Center

This section contains practical information about getting to Boston and traveling around once you are there, as well as tips, useful phone numbers, money matters and public holidays.

Planning Ahead	**114–115**
Getting There	**116–117**
Getting Around	**118–119**
Essential Facts	**120–123**
Timeline	**124–125**

Planning Ahead

When to Go

Summer and fall are peak visiting seasons. Hotels are busy at graduation time (May, June) and rates go up. In October you will get a glimpse of New England's fall foliage (better still farther north). The time between Thanksgiving and New Year is full of seasonal festivities.

AVERAGE DAILY MAXIMUM TEMPERATURES

JAN	FEB	MAR	APR	MAY	JUN	JUL	AUG	SEP	OCT	NOV	DEC
37°F	37°F	46°F	56°F	66°F	76°F	82°F	80°F	75°F	63°F	52°F	37°F
3°C	3°C	8°C	13°C	19°C	24°C	28°C	26°C	24°C	17°C	11°C	3°C

Spring (April through May) is unpredictable, but can be wonderful, with cool nights and fresh days. This is when you can catch the magnolia blossoms in Back Bay.

Summer (June through August) is normally pleasantly warm, but occasional heatwaves can see temperatures soaring into the 90s.

Fall (September through November) is warm in September and crisp in October and November, when the foliage is at its most colorful.

Winter (December through March) is very cold. Even when the sky is blue winds can be biting. Snows occasionally transform the city; a slushy, gray mess inevitably follows.

WHAT'S ON

January *Martin Luther King weekend.*

February *Chinese New Year* (Jan/Feb).

March *Spring Flower Show. St. Patrick's Day Parade.*

April *Patriots' Day* (3rd Mon): Revere's Ride is re-created.

Boston Marathon (3rd Mon). *Kite Festival* (or May): held in Franklin Park.

May *May Fair* in Harvard Square.

Boston Pops Concerts.

June *Battle of Bunker Hill*: re-enactment (Sun before Bunker Hill Day, Jun 17).

Cambridge River Festival: Events on the river.

July *Boston Pops Concerts. Independence celebrations* (week of Jul 4): Boston Pops concert with fireworks, Boston Harborfest music festival and USS *Constitution* turnaround.

Italian Feste (festivals, Jul/Aug weekends): North End.

August *Moon Festival*: Processions in Chinatown.

September *Boston Arts Festival*: Columbus Waterfront.

Boston Symphony Orchestra: Season Sep–May.

October *Columbus Day Parade.*

Head of the Charles Regatta (3rd week).

November *Christmas tree lighting ceremonies*: Faneuil Hall Marketplace and Charles Square, Cambridge.

Boston Ballet—The Nutcracker (Nov–Dec): Boston Opera House.

December *Tree lighting ceremonies*: Prudential Center, Harvard Square.

Boston Tea Party (mid-Dec): Re-enactment.

Carol concert: Trinity Church. *First Night*: New Year's Eve.

Boston Online

www.boston.com
The *Boston Globe*'s website has the daily newspaper, with local news, listings and restaurant reviews.

www.boston.citysearch.com
A guide to local events, theater productions, movies, concerts, sports, stores and restaurants. The site tends to feature the big-name destinations and happenings, so you'll find everything from top-10 restaurant lists and heavy-hitter museum exhibits to addresses, phone numbers, schedules and maps.

www.thephoenix.com
The *Boston Phoenix* is a weekly alternative newspaper that offers detailed arts and entertainment listings, plus restaurant reviews.

www.bostonusa.com
Run by the Greater Boston Convention and Visitors Bureau, this site includes details about attractions, events, hotels and the subway, as well as other useful visitor information.

www.cambridge-usa.org
This is the Cambridge Office for Tourism's site and it contains listings of hotels, restaurants, attractions and arts and entertainment venues, as well as an events calendar and general visitor information for the City of Cambridge.

www.dailycandy.com/boston
Click onto the Boston edition of this national site to find listings for the city's brand new restaurants and hottest stores, eclectic shows and services and other undiscovered gems.

www.mbta.com
The website of the MBTA (Massachusetts Bay Transportation Authority) is the place to look for timetables, maps and fare information for the T (subway), as well as commuter rail services and buses.

PRIME TRAVEL SITES

www.fodors.com
A complete travel-planning site. You can research prices and weather; book air tickets, cars and rooms; ask questions (and get answers) from fellow travelers; and find links to other sites.

www.massvacation.com
Visitor information from the Massachusetts Office of Travel and Tourism. The site includes an accommodation booking service.

www.orbitz.com
An air-fare search engine owned by five US airlines. It frequently offers low-fare specials.

www.discovernewengland.org
This is the official site for the states of New England, if you are planning a visit beyond Boston.

INTERNET CAFÉ

FedEx Kinko's
Copy and printing shops that offer internet access. Locations include:

🞢 F5 ✉ 187 Dartmouth Street (Back Bay) ☎ 617/262-6188 🕐 24 hours 🚇 Back Bay Station, Copley ✋ $15 per hour

🞢 C2 ✉ Mifflin Place (off Mt. Auburn Street, Harvard Square) ☎ 617/497-0125 🕐 24 hours 🚇 Harvard ✋ $15 per hour

Getting There

ENTRY REQUIREMENTS

International travelers going to the US under the Visa Waiver Program (VWP) are now subject to enhanced security requirements. Online completion and approval of ESTA (Electronic System for Travel Authorization), along with payment of the fee, is mandatory ahead of travel for all VWP travelers. For full details, go to the official website https://esta.cbp.dhs.gov.

CAR RENTAL

Logan Airport has 10 car rental companies operating within it; reserve in advance.

Alamo
www.alamo.com
☎ 877/222-9075

Avis
www.avis.com
☎ 800/633-3469

Budget
www.budget.com
☎ 800/218-7992

Dollar
www.dollar.com
☎ 800/800-4000

Enterprise
www.enterprise.com
☎ 800/325-8007

Hertz
www.hertz.com
☎ 800/654-3131

National
www.nationalcar.com
☎ 877/222-9058

Thrifty
www.thrifty.com
☎ 800/847-4389

AIRPORTS

Logan Airport is on an island in Boston Harbor. It has four terminals, hotels and restaurants. Domestic flights also use T. F. Green Airport (Rhode Island), Manchester Airport (New Hampshire) and Worcester Airport (Massachusetts).

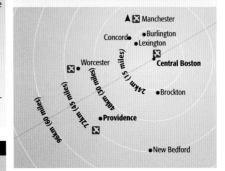

FROM LOGAN AIRPORT

For general airport information ☎ 800/235-6426. "Massport Shuttle" buses run every 20 minutes (5.30am–1am; free) from every terminal to Airport subway (T) station; from here it's a few minutes' journey to central Boston ($2).

Taxis cost $25–$45 (including a tunnel toll, but not tip). Thanks to the new Massachusetts Turnpike extensions from Logan, travel time to and from the airport has been reduced dramatically. Allow roughly 15–25 minutes to or from Back Bay (▷ panel, opposite).

Harbor Express (☎ 617/222-6999) is an exciting way to arrive in central Boston. It's a 10-minute boat ride between Logan and Long Wharf in the Financial District, where you can pick up a taxi. Harbor Express also operates between Logan and Quincy and Hull, on the south shore (Mon–Fri 5.55am–11pm, Sat 8am–10pm, Sun 8am–9pm; $10 to Long Wharf). An on-call City Water Taxi (☎ 617/422-0392) runs all year from Logan to 15 different waterfront locations (Mon–Sat 7am–10pm, Sun 7am–8pm; $10). Shuttle buses connect all terminals with the water taxis.

OTHER AIRPORTS

Domestic flights also use T. F. Green Airport, Rhode Island (☎ 401/737-8222); Manchester Airport, New Hampshire (☎ 603/624-6539); and Worcester Airport, Massachusetts (☎ 508/799-1350). It's then more than an hour's bus ride to Boston.

ARRIVING BY BUS

Greyhound (☎ 800/231-2222) and Peter Pan Trailways (☎ 800/343-9999) travel between New York and Boston's South Station, and (less frequently) to the rest of the USA and Canada.

ARRIVING BY CAR

Boston can be a difficult city to drive in for visitors, and parking is scarce. The Big Dig highway construction project, which reorganized highways into and through Boston, is now complete. If you do drive, select a hotel with free parking, get a good map and plan your route. The major east-west highway into Boston is the I-90 toll road, also known as the Massachusetts Turnpike. I-90 links up with I-93 just south of downtown. I-93 is the major north-south highway, and it travels through tunnels under downtown Boston. I-95, the East Coast's major north-south interstate highway, circles the perimeter of the Boston metropolitan area.

ARRIVING BY TRAIN

Amtrak (☎ 800/872-7245; www.amtrak.com) runs a frequent service between Boston's South Station and Providence, New York, Philadelphia and Washington, D.C. The high-speed Acela service between New York and Boston takes three and a half hours. South Station also serves Washington, D.C. and Chicago. Amtrak's Down-easter travels up the coast to Maine from North Station. Trains running within New England tend to arrive and depart on time, but those traveling longer distances are frequently delayed—particularly in winter, when snow slows them down—usually anywhere from 10 minutes to an hour.

TIME TO LOGAN

From downtown Boston, driving to Logan averages 15 minutes. However, during heavy traffic hours (generally 7.30–9.30am and 4.30–6pm on weekdays), count on the ride taking 30 minutes, possibly even 40 in the dead of rush hour. Security lines on international flights can also be quite long, so plan accordingly.

EATING ON THE RUN

At Logan Airport, find:
Legal Sea Foods (you can also buy live lobsters to take home with you).
Wolfgang Puck, quick and healthy pizzas.
Todd English's Bonfire, new American cooking from one of New England's top chefs.
Boston Beer Works, micro-brews and American food.
Johnny Rockets, American burgers, shakes and jukebox.
Fresh City, wrap sandwiches to go.
Starbucks, for fresh-ground coffee, lattes and sandwiches.

In South Station, find:
Rosie's Bakery, for rich fudges, cakes and brownies.
Au Bon Pain, sandwiches, soups and salads.
Pizzeria Regina, locally loved, small Italian chain.
Surf City Squeeze, for fresh-made fruit smoothies.

Getting Around

BICYCLES

Boston is now attempting to become a bicycle-friendly town. Meanwhile, if you are looking to get some exercise outside the city, Boston has several bicycle paths that offer pleasant riding. One is the Southwest Corridor, which runs from behind the Massachusetts Avenue T stop as far as the Arnold Arboretum in Jamaica Plain. A longer ride is the Minuteman Bikeway, which runs from Alewife Station in Cambridge all the way out to Bedford—passing by the historical sites in Lexington (▷ 106) on the way.

VISITORS WITH DISABILITIES

An Airport Handicap Van offers a free service between all Logan Airport locations. Use the free "Van Phone" in the baggage-claim area. Public buildings, parking areas and most subway stations provide wheelchair access, and many hotels have specially designed rooms. Modern or newly renovated hotels and restaurants tend to be better equipped. For further information contact: New England INDEX ✉ 200 Trapelo Road, Waltham, MA 02452 ☎ 781/642-0248; www.disabilityinfo.org

VISITOR PASSES

● An MBTA (Massachusetts Bay Transportation Authority) Link Pass gives unlimited travel for one or seven days ($11, $18) on all subways, buses and ferries. It is available at vending machines in T stations and online in advance at www.mbta.com. It is NOT available at visitor information centers.

BOATS

● MBTA ferry/Boston Harbor cruises (☎ 617/227-4321) link Long Wharf and Charlestown, Long Wharf and Provincetown.

BUSES

● Buses travel farther out into the suburbs than the T, but the T is much quicker and easier in the center.
● Passengers must have the exact change ($1.50) or Charlie Card. Express Bus has an additional charge.
● For travel farther afield, bus companies operate out of South Station serving destinations throughout New England.

SUBWAY (T)

● Boston's system of subway and elevated trains is known as the T. The five lines—Red, Green, Orange, Silver and Blue—meet in central Boston. "Inbound" and "Outbound" refer to direction in relation to Park Street Station.
● The clean and efficient trains run from 5am (later on Sunday) to 1am.
● Rides are now by Charlie Cards, reloadable cards bought at vending machines in stations. Individual rides are $2 or $2.50, depending on the plan selected. These machines are not especially easy for the first-time user, so it is a good idea to visit www.mbta.com in advance, for a clear explanation of the options and operation of machines.
● Free maps are available at the Park Street Station information booth. There is also a T map on the inside flap at the front of this book.

TAXIS
● Hail taxis on the street or find them at hotels and taxi stands.
● 24-hour taxi services include:
Yellow Cab ☎ 617/621-2500
Metrocab Cab ☎ 617/782-5500
Town Taxis ☎ 617/536-5000

TRAINS
● MBTA commuter trains leave from North Station for destinations west and north, including Lowell, Concord, Salem, Manchester, Gloucester, Rockport and Ipswich. South Station serves Plymouth and Providence.

DRIVING AND CAR RENTAL
Car rental
● Rental drivers must be at least 21; many companies put the minimum age at 25 or charge extra for those between 21 and 25.
● For car rental companies, ▷ 116.
● Consider using the subway to pick up your car from a rental agency on the outskirts of Boston to avoid having to drive in the city.

Driving
● Driving and parking in Boston is challenging.
● Park only in legal spots, or you will be towed. Park in the direction of the traffic.
● Speed limits on the major highways range from 55 to 65mph (90 to 104kph); elsewhere they range from 30 to 45mph (48 to 72kph).
● All passengers must wear a seat belt. Children under 12 years old must sit in the back and use an approved car seat or safety belt.
● You may turn right at a red traffic light if the road ahead is clear, unless signage prohibits it.
● Drink/driving laws are strict. Never drive after drinking; don't keep opened alcohol in the car.
● Look out for one-way streets, especially in downtown Boston where they are legion. Boston taxi drivers are aggressive—the best defense is to yield whenever necessary. And don't be afraid to use your horn!

PEDICABS
A fun and efficient alternative to taxis and subways are the "cycle rickshaws" run by Boston Pedicab (617/266-2005; www.bostonpedicab.com). The bicycle cabs are easy to find Downtown and can take you to where you are going quickly.

TAXI FARES
At the time of publication, taxi rates are $2.60 for the first 1/7 mile (0.23km), and $0.40 for each additional 1/7 mile (0.23km); or $28 for each hour spent waiting. (Be sure to check rates at the airport.) Trips to and from the airport are subject to additional tolls of $2.75 and $8, respectively; there is no charge for luggage. For trips beyond 12 miles (20km) from downtown Boston, a flat-rate applies: www.cityofboston.gov

NEED TO KNOW GETTING AROUND

Essential Facts

TRAVEL INSURANCE

It is vital to have cover for medical expenses, as well as for theft, baggage loss, trip cancellation and accidents. Check your insurance coverage and buy a supplementary policy as needed.

MONEY

The currency is the dollar (=100 cents). Notes (bills) are in denominations of $1, $5, $10, $20, $50 and $100; coins are 25¢ (a quarter), 10¢ (a dime), 5¢ (a nickel) and 1¢ (a penny). You may find that small businesses will not break a $100, $50 or even $20 bill.

ALCOHOL

● It is illegal to drink alcohol in public places such as the T. Do not keep opened bottles of alcohol in the car.
● It is illegal to sell alcohol to anyone under the age of 21. Alcohol is on sale daily, 12–8 on Sunday.

MAGAZINES AND NEWSPAPERS

● Free tourist magazines are found in hotel lobbies, and include discount coupons.
● Listings can be found in the *Boston Globe* (Thursday), the *Boston Herald* (Friday) and the *Boston Phoenix*.
● *Boston Magazine* (monthly) reviews the Boston scene and gives awards to restaurants. Also online: www.bostonmagazine.com.

MAIL

● Letter boxes are gray/blue and have swing-top lids. Most hotels will mail letters for you.

MONEY MATTERS

● Nearly all banks have Automatic Teller Machines. Cards registered in other countries that are linked to the Cirrus or Plus networks are accepted. Before leaving, check which network your cards are linked to and ensure your PIN is valid in the US, where four-figure numbers are the norm.
● Credit cards are widely accepted.
● US dollar traveler's checks function like cash in larger hotels and stores.
● Money and traveler's checks can be exchanged at most banks (check fees as they can be high) and many travel centers in central Boston.
● Some businesses may ask for photo identification before cashing traveler's checks.

OPENING HOURS

● Banks: Mon–Fri 9–4, Thu 9–5 or later, Sat 9–12.
● Shops: Mon–Sat 10–6 or later. Sun mornings from 11am.

● Museums and sights: Unless otherwise stated, all sights mentioned in this book close on Thanksgiving and Christmas.
● Businesses: Mon–Fri 8 or 9–5.

PUBLIC HOLIDAYS
● **Jan 1** (New Year's Day)
● **3rd Mon in Jan** (Martin Luther King Day)
● **3rd Mon in Feb** (President's Day)
● **Last Mon in May** (Memorial Day)
● **July 4** (Independence Day)
● **1st Mon in Sep** (Labor Day)
● **2nd Mon in Oct** (Columbus Day)
● **Nov 11** (Veterans Day)
● **4th Thu in Nov** (Thanksgiving)
● **Dec 25** (Christmas Day)
● Boston also celebrates: **Mar 17** (Evacuation Day); **3rd Mon in Apr** (Patriots' Day); **Jun 17** (Bunker Hill Day).

SENSIBLE PRECAUTIONS
● Boston is basically a safe city, but it is wise to stick to well-lit and well-populated areas after dark. Avoid the lower half of Washington Street and Boston Common at night.
● Discuss your itinerary with your hotel's reception staff so they can point out any potential problems. Be aware of the people around you, especially at night or in quiet areas.
● Keep your wallet or purse out of sight and don't carry valuables or cash openly.
● Do not carry easily snatched bags and cameras, or put your wallet into your back pocket.
● Keep valuables in your hotel's safe and never carry more money than you need.
● Lost traveler's checks are relatively quick and easy to replace. Keep the numbers of the checks separate from the checks themselves.
● Report any stolen item to the nearest police station, if only to be able to claim on your insurance. The police will fill out the forms your insurance company will need.
● Always lock car doors and keep valuables out of sight.

SMOKING
● Smoking is banned in restaurants unless there is a separate seating area. It is banned in many public places, including the T. Some hotels have no-smoking floors.
● Cambridge is by law smoke-free.

LOST AND FOUND

● To report lost credit cards:
American Express
☎ 800/528-4800;
Diners Club/Carte Blanche
☎ 800/234-6377;
MasterCard
☎ 800/627-8372;
Visa ☎ 800/847-2911
● Lost traveler's checks:
American Express
☎ 800/221-7282

PARKING

If you plan on driving in
Boston, note that the city is
notorious for its lack of parking. That said, follow these
tips, and you should do fine:
● Look for public parking
garages. Though more costly,
these are by far the most
convenient, as they are plen-
tiful (especially Downtown).
The garage under the
Common is the most eco-
nomical at $28 for 24 hours,
$10 for additional hours.
● Allow extra time. Some
destinations have garages
and/or valet, some don't.
If the latter, circle until you
get lucky enough to find an
empty spot on the street.
Look for side streets but be
careful not to park in "residents only" streets (which
are the majority).
● Pay attention to parking
signs on the street. Boston's
meter maids are merciless.

STUDENT TRAVELERS

● To get discounts on the T and admissions, get
an International Student Identity Card (ISIC). If
you are not a student but are under 26, get the
International Youth Travel Card (IYTC).
● The Council on International Educational
Exchange (CIEE) has a travel service offering
domestic passes for bargain travel within the
US. It is also the exclusive agent for several
student-discount cards: ✉ 300 Fore Street,
Portland, Maine ☎ 888/268-6245.
● Members of the Youth Hostel Association
of England and Wales (✉ Trevelyan House,
Dimple Road, Matlock, Derbyshire DE4 3YH
☎ 01629 592600) can use Hi-Boston hostels.
● Information on student hostels within the US
can be obtained from Hostelling International–
USA (✉ 8401 Colesville Road, Suite 600,
Silver Spring, MD 20910 ☎ 240/650-2100;
fax 240/650-2094; email: info@hihostels.com;
www.hihostels.com).

TELEPHONES

● The area codes for Boston and Cambridge
are 617 and 857. These must be included
even when making local calls. Some communi-
ties outside the city have different area codes.
● To call the US from the UK dial 00 1,
followed by the area code and the number.
● To call the UK from the US, dial 011 44, then
drop the initial zero from the area code.

TICKETS

● The nine-day Boston CityPASS (adult $51;
seniors and children ages 3–11 $36) gives
free admission for one visit each at five key
sights: the Museum of Fine Arts (▷ 70–71),
the Museum of Science (▷ 28–29), the New
England Aquarium (▷ 53), either the Old State
House (▷ 103) or Harvard Museum of Natural
History (▷ 91), and Skywalk Observatory
(▷ 73). Available from the above sights or
at the visitor information center on Boston
Common (▷ 50), in the Prudential Center

(▷ 73) or on its website www.citypass.com/city/boston.

TOURIST OFFICES
● **Greater Boston Convention & Visitors Bureau Inc.** ✉ 2 Copley Place, Suite 105, Boston, MA 02116 ☎ 617/ 536-4100; fax 617/424-7664; www.bostonusa.com
● **Massachusetts Office of Travel & Tourism** ✉ State Transportation Building, 10 Park Plaza, Suite 4510, Boston, MA 02116 ☎ 617/973-8500; fax 617/973-8525; www.massvacation.com
● **Boston National Historical Park Visitor Center** ✉ 15 State Street, opposite Old State House ☎ 617/242-5642
● **Boston Common Visitor Center** ✉ 139 Tremont Street ☎ 617/426-3115
● **Cambridge Office for Tourism** ✉ 4 Brattle Street, Harvard Square, Cambridge ☎ 617/441-2884; www.cambridgeusa.org

EMERGENCY MEDICAL TREATMENT

Ambulance, fire, police	☎ 911
Massachusetts General Hospital	☎ 617/726-2000
Inn-House Doctor	☎ 617/859-1776 🕐 24 hours. Makes hotel visits
Late-night pharmacies: CVS	✉ Porter Square (35 White Street, near Massachusetts Avenue), Cambridge ☎ 617/876-5519 🕐 24 hours
	✉ 587 Boylston Street, Back Bay ☎ 617/437-8414 🕐 24 hours
Dental emergency	☎ 617/636-6828
Eye and Ear Infirmary	☎ 617/523-7900
Physician Referral Service	☎ 617/726-5800 🕐 Mon–Fri 8.30–4.45

CONSULATES

Canada	✉ 3 Copley Place ☎ 617/247-51000
Great Britain	✉ 1 Broadway, Cambridge ☎ 617/245-4500
Ireland	✉ 535 Boylston Street ☎ 617/267-9330
Italy	✉ 600 Atlantic Avenue ☎ 617/722-9201
Portugal	✉ 699 Boylston Street ☎ 617/536-8740
Spain	✉ 31 St. James Avenue ☎ 617/536-2506

Timeline

REVOLUTION

In the 1760s Britain imposed taxes on her New England colonists. Increasingly angry at interference in their lucrative seafaring trade, the colonists, led by Sons of Freedom Sam Adams and John Hancock, protested at having to pay taxes when they had no representation in the government that was taxing them. Tension began to mount and on March 5, 1770 British soldiers killed five colonists in what became known as the Boston Massacre. On December 16, 1773, Patriots protested against the Tea Act by throwing tea into the sea (the Boston Tea Party). British retaliation made clashes inevitable.

From left: American Revolution re-enactment; statue of a Minute Man on the spot where events sparked the revolution; plaque on the grave of Samuel Adams; equestrian statue of Paul Revere; obelisk commemorating the Battle of Bunker Hill, June 17, 1775

Pre–1620 The Algonquins inhabit the Boston area.

1620 Pilgrims arrive on the *Mayflower* and establish the first English colony in Plymouth.

1629 Puritans found the Massachusetts Bay Colony in Charlestown.

1630 The colony moves to Beacon Hill on the Shawmut Peninsula.

1636 Harvard College is founded.

1680 Most of Boston is concentrated in what is to become the North End, around the flourishing seaport.

1775 The Revolution starts in Boston.

1776 The British leave Boston on March 17. On July 18, the Declaration of Independence is read from the State House balcony.

1790s Trade with China brings prosperity.

1795 Architect Charles Bulfinch starts the new State House. Five years later he helps to develop Beacon Hill.

1826 Mayor Josiah Quincy extends the waterfront and builds Quincy Market.

1840s Irish immigrants, fleeing the Potato Famine, pour into the North End.

1856 Work begins on filling in and developing the Back Bay as a new residential area.

1897 The Boston Marathon is launched. John J. McDermott of New York wins.

1918 The Red Sox win baseball's World Series—their first pennant victory. Their next victory was not to be until 2004.

1960s–70s An extensive urban renewal scheme includes John Hancock Tower.

1990 The US's biggest art theft occurs at the Isabella Stewart Gardner Museum.

2004 New England Patriots win the Super Bowl for the second time since 2002. The Boston Red Sox win the World Series championship for the first time in almost a century.

2006 The Big Dig, Boston's decade-long, large-scale construction project to ease Boston's huge traffic problem, finally ends.

2009 Senator Edward Kennedy, the political face of Massachusetts on the national and international scene for over 40 years, dies.

2013 The motto "Boston Strong" goes round the world after the April 15 Boston Marathon bombings that killed three and injured more than 250. The city's beloved Boston Red Sox respond by winning the World Series for the eighth time.

PAUL REVERE'S RIDE

In his lifetime Paul Revere (1735–1818) was known as a silversmith, but he was immortalized—with some poetic license—as a hero of the Revolution by the poet Henry Wadsworth Longfellow. Revere was a messenger for the Sons of Liberty and on the eve of the first battle of the Revolution rode to Lexington to warn local militia men about British preparations.

JFK

John Fitzgerald Kennedy was born in the Boston suburb of Brookline in 1917. His grandfather, "Honey-Fitz," was one of a long line of Irish mayors. Kennedy was elected president in 1960—good-looking and charismatic, he was a symbol of the nation's hope for a progressive future. He was assassinated on November 22, 1963.

Index

A

accommodations 107–112
  bed-and-breakfast 109, 111
  hotels 109–112
Adams Gallery 54
African Meeting House 25, 38
airports 116–117
alcohol 82, 119, 120
Ames Building 38
Arlington Street Church 54
Arnold Arboretum 17, 104
art and antiques 10, 12, 41, 42, 72, 94
Arthur M. Sackler Museum 91

B

Back Bay 67
Back Bay and the South End 63–84
  entertainment and nightlife 82–83
  map 64–65
  restaurants 84
  shopping 72, 80–81
  sights 66–78
  walk 79
ballet and modern dance 18, 60, 96
banks 120
baseball 5, 78
Beacon Hill 8, 24–25
Beacon Hill to Charlestown 20–46
  entertainment and nightlife 43
  map 22–23
  restaurants 45–46
  shopping 41–42
  sights 24–39
  walk 40
bed-and-breakfast 109, 111
bicycle paths 118
Black Heritage Trail 39
book stores 10, 12, 58, 94, 95
Boston Athenaeum 54
Boston Children's Museum 18, 54
Boston Common 8, 50
Boston Common to the Waterfront 47–62
  entertainment and nightlife 59–60
  map 48–49
  restaurants 61–62
  shopping 58
  sights 50–56
  walk 57
Boston environs 99–106
  excursions 105–106
  map 100–101

sights 102–104
Boston Fire Museum 54
Boston Harbor Islands 9, 102
Boston Public Library 9, 66, 82
Boston Tea Party Ships and Museum 51
Boston Women's Memorial 17, 67
Brattle Street 92
budget travelers 18, 109
Bulfinch, Charles 24, 27, 35, 39
Bumpkin Island 102
Bunker Hill Monument 37
Busch-Reisinger Museum 91
buses 117, 118

C

Cambridge 85–98
  entertainment and nightlife 96–97
  map 86–87
  restaurants 97–98
  shopping 94–95
  sights 88–92
  walk 93
car rental 116, 119
Charles River 38, 78
Charles Street 41, 42
Charlestown 36–37
Cheers 43
children 12, 18
Chinatown 13, 14, 55, 57, 62
Christopher Columbus Waterfront Park 38
cinema 83, 96
climate and seasons 114
clubs and bars 13
  see *also* entertainment and nightlife
comedy clubs 43, 59, 60
Commonwealth Avenue 9, 67
Concord 106
consulates 123
Copp's Hill Burying Ground 31
crafts 11, 12, 42, 80, 94
credit cards 120, 122
Custom House Tower 17, 38

D

dental treatment 123
department stores 12, 80, 81
disabilities, visitors with 118
driving 117, 119, 122

E

eating out 14
  see *also* restaurants
Emerald Necklace 4, 67, 78, 104

entertainment and nightlife 13
  Back Bay and the South End 82–83
  Beacon Hill to Charlestown 43
  Boston Common to the Waterfront 59–60
  Cambridge 96–97
Esplanade 16, 38, 78
events and festivals 114
excursions 105–106

F

Faneuil Hall and Marketplace 9, 26, 41
fashion shopping 10, 11, 12, 16, 41, 42, 58, 72, 80, 81, 95, 96
Fens 17, 78
Fenway Park 78
First Church of Christ, Scientist 78
Fogg Art Museum 91
food and drink
  alcohol 82, 119, 120
  baked beans 10, 46
  New England dishes 46
  seafood 18, 45, 46, 61, 62, 98
  shopping for 12, 41, 42, 94, 95
  vegetarian food 15, 62
  see *also* eating out; restaurants
Fort Warren 102
Franklin Park Zoo 104
Frederick Law Olmsted National Historic Site 104

G

Georges Island 102
gifts and souvenirs 10, 12
Gillette Stadium 104
Granary Burying Ground 40, 55
Grape Island 102

H

Harrison Gray Otis House 9, 27
Harvard Museum of Natural History (HMNH) 91
Harvard Square 9, 89, 93, 94–95
Harvard University 4, 9, 88–89
Harvard University museums 9, 90–91
history 124–125
hostels 122
hotels 109–112

I

Institute of Contemporary Art (ICA) 52
insurance 120
internet access 123

internet café 115
Irish Famine Memorial 55
Isabella Stewart Gardner
    Museum 9, 16, 68–69

J
James Curley statue 38
JFK Library and Museum
    9, 103
JFK National Historic Site 104
John Hancock Tower 17, 77

K
Kennedy, J. F. 103, 104, 125
King's Chapel and Burying
    Ground 55

L
Larz Anderson Auto Museum 104
Lexington 106
licensing laws 82, 120
Longfellow House 92
lost property 122
Louisburg Square 24
Lovells Island 102

M
Mapparium 78
maps
    Back Bay and the South End
        64–65
    Beacon Hill to Charlestown
        22–23
    Boston Common to the
        Waterfront 48–49
    Boston environs 100–101
    Cambridge 86–87
    Mayflower II 105
medical treatment 123
MIT buildings 92
MIT sculptures 92
money 120
Mount Auburn Cemetery 92
Museum of African American
    History 39
Museum of Fine Arts 9, 18,
    70–71, 83
museum opening hours 121
museum pass 122–123
Museum of Science 9, 18,
    28–29
music venues 43, 59, 60, 82, 83,
    96, 97

N
New England Aquarium 9, 16,
    18, 53
New England Holocaust
    Memorial 39

Newbury Street 8, 10, 11, 72,
    80, 81
newspapers and magazines
    120
Nichols House Museum 25, 39
North End 8, 13, 30–31, 34

O
Old North Church 8, 31
Old South Meeting House 56
Old State House 8, 32–33
opening hours 120–121
outdoor gear and clothing 12,
    42, 58, 80, 81

P
Park Street Church 56
parking 119, 122
passports and visas 116
Paul Revere House 8, 34
Paul Revere Mall 31
Paul Revere statue 39
Peabody Museum 91
Peabody Essex Museum 106
Peddocks Island 102
pedicabs 119
pharmacies 123
Pilgrim Hall Museum 105
Plimoth Plantation 105
Plymouth 105
Plymouth National Wax
    Museum 105
Plymouth Rock 105
Post Office Square 56
Prudential Center 8, 73, 81
Prudential Tower 17, 73
Public Garden 6, 16, 17, 50
public holidays 121
public transportation 115,
    118–119

Q
Quincy Market, see Faneuil
    Hall Marketplace

R
restaurants 13, 14, 15
    Back Bay and the South End 84
    Beacon Hill to Charlestown
        45–46
    Boston Common to the
        Waterfront 61–62
    Cambridge 97–98
Revere, Paul 34, 35, 39, 55,
    106, 125
river tours 38, 43
Robert Gould Shaw Memorial
    17, 56

S
safety, personal 121
Salem 106
Samuel Adams statue 39
Sears Building 38
shopping 10–12, 16
    Back Bay and the South End
        72, 80–81
    Beacon Hill to Charlestown
        41–42
    Boston Common to the
        Waterfront 58
    Cambridge 94–95
skyscrapers 17
Skywalk 8, 13, 73
Sleepy Hollow Cemetery 106
smoking etiquette 121
South End 8, 74–75
SoWa district 75
State House 8, 35
student travelers 122
subway system 118

T
taxis 119
TD Garden 39
telephones 122
theater 18, 43, 59, 60, 82, 83,
    96, 97
ticket outlets 59
time differences 114
tourist information 115, 123
train services 117, 119
traveler's checks 120, 121, 122
Trinity Church 8, 16, 76–77

U
USS Constitution 8, 36–37

V
views over the city 17, 38, 73
visitor passes 118, 122–123

W
walks
    Beacon Hill 40
    Boston Common to the
        Waterfront 57
    Harvard Square 93
    South End 79
Wampanoag Homesite 105
websites 115
whale-watching 16, 53

Z
zoo 104

Boston 25 Best

WRITTEN BY Sue Gordon
ADDITIONAL WRITING Alexandra Hall and Michael Blanding
UPDATED BY Andrew Church
SERIES EDITOR Clare Ashton
COVER DESIGN Chie Ushio, Yuko Inagaki
DESIGN WORK Tracey Freestone, Nick Johnston
IMAGE RETOUCHING AND REPRO Ian Little

Published in the United Kingdom by AA Publishing

ISBN 978-0-8041-4340-0

EIGHTH EDITION

SPECIAL SALES
This book is available for special discounts for bulk purchases for sales promotions or premiums. For more information, email specialmarkets@randomhouse.com.

Color separation by AA Digital Department
Printed and bound by Leo Paper Products, China

10 9 8 7 6 5 4 3 2 1

A05141
Maps in this title produced from mapping © MAIRDUMONT / Falk Verlag 2013
Transport map © Communicarta Ltd, UK

The Automobile Association wishes to thank the following photographers, companies and picture libraries for their assistance in the preparation of this book.

Abbreviations for the picture credits are as follows – (t) top; (b) bottom; (l) left; (r) right; (c) center; (AA) AA World Travel Library.

1 AA/J Nicholson; **2** AA/M Lynch; **3** AA/M Lynch; **4t** AA/M Lynch; **4c** AA/M Lynch; **5t** AA/M Lynch; **5c** AA/C Sawyer; **6t** AA/M Lynch; **6cl** AA/C Sawyer; **6c** AA/M Lynch; **6cr** AA/M Lynch; **6bl** AA/C Sawyer; **6bcl** AA/C Sawyer; **6bcr** AA/C Coe; **6br** Photodisc; **7t** AA/M Lynch; **7cl** AA/J Nicholson; **7cr** AA/C Sawyer; **7bl** AA/M Lynch; **7bc** AA/J Nicholson; **7br** AA/M Lynch; **8** AA/M Lynch; **9** AA/M Lynch; **10t** AA/M Lynch; **10ct** AA/C Sawyer; **10c** AA/C Sawyer; **10/11cb** AA/D Clapp; **10/11b** AA/C Coe; **11t** AA/M Lynch; **11ct** AA/M Lynch; **11c** AA/C Sawyer; **12** AA/M Lynch; **13t** AA/M Lynch; **13tct** AA/C Sawyer; **13ct** AA/J Nicholson; **13c** AA/D Clapp; **13cb** Brand X Pictures ; **13b** AA/M Lynch; **14t** AA/M Lynch; **14ct** AA/C Sawyer; **14c** AA/C Sawyer; **14cb** AA/C Sawyer; **14b** AA/C Sawyer; **15t** AA/M Lynch; **15b** AA/D Clapp; **16t** AA/M Lynch; **16ct** AA/M Lynch; **16c** AA/C Sawyer; **16cb** AA/C Sawyer; **16b** AA/J Nicholson; **17t** AA/M Lynch; **17ct** AA/C Sawyer; **17c** AA/M Lynch; **17cb** AA/C Sawyer; **17b** AA/C Sawyer; **18t** AA/M Lynch; **18ct** AA/C Sawyer; **18c** AA/J Nicholson; **18cb** AA/C Sawyer; **18b** AA/P Kenward; **19t** AA/J Nicholson; **19ct** AA/C Sawyer; **19c** AA/J Nicholson; **19cb** AA/C Coe; **19b** AA/C Sawyer; **20/21** AA/D Clapp; **24tl** AA/C Sawyer; **24cl** AA/C Sawyer; **24cr** AA/C Sawyer; **24/25t** AA/C Coe; **24/25c** AA/C Coe; **25r** AA/J Nicholson; **26l** AA/C Sawyer; **26r** AA/J Nicholson; **27l** AA/C Sawyer; **27r** AA/C Sawyer; **28l** AA/C Sawyer; **28/29t** AA/C Sawyer; **28/29b** AA/C Sawyer; **29tr** Courtesy of Boston Museum of Science; **29bl** AA/D Clapp; **29br** AA/D Clapp; **30** AA/C Sawyer; **30/31** AA/C Sawyer; **31** AA/M Lynch; **32** AA/J Nicholson; **32/33** AA/C Sawyer; **34l** AA/J Nicholson; **34c** AA/C Sawyer; **34r** AA/C Coe; **35l** AA/J Nicholson; **35r** AA/C Coe; **36** AA/C Coe; **36/37t** AA/C Sawyer; **36/37b** AA/J Nicholson; **37l** AA/C Coe; **37r** AA/J Nicholson; **38t** AA/C Sawyer; **38bl** Courtesy of Greater Boston Convention & Visitors Bureau; **38br** AA/C Sawyer; **39t** AA/C Sawyer; **39bl** AA/J Nicholson; **39br** Courtesy of Museum of African American History; **40** AA/J Nicholson; **41** AA/D Clapp; **42** AA/C Sawyer; **43** Digital Vision; **44** Photodisc; **45** AA/C Sawyer; **46** AA/C Sawyer; **47** AA/D Clapp; **50l** Image Management/Alamy; **50r** Visual Mining/Alamy; **51** AA/C Sawyer; **52l** Courtesy of Institute of Contemporary Art/Boston; **52r** Courtesy of Institute of Contemporary Art/Boston; **53l** AA/C Sawyer; **53r** AA/C Sawyer; **54t** AA/C Sawyer; **54b** AA/C Sawyer; **55t** AA/C Sawyer; **55b** AA/C Sawyer; **56t** AA/C Sawyer; **56bl** Courtesy of Old South Meeting House; **56br** AA/C Sawyer; **57** AA/J Nicholson; **58** AA/S McBride; **59** Digital Vision; **60** Brand X pictures **61** AA/P Bennett; **62** Bananastock; **63** AA/C Coe; **66l** AA/C Sawyer; **66r** AA/C Sawyer; **67l** AA/C Sawyer; **67r** AA/C Coe; **68/69** Courtesy of Isabella Stewart Gardner Museum; **69** Courtesy of Isabella Stewart Gardner Museum; **70** Courtesy of Museum of Fine Arts; **70/71** AA/C Sawyer; **72l** AA/C Sawyer; **72r** AA/C Sawyer; **73l** AA/J Nicholson; **73c** AA/C Sawyer; **73r** AA/D Clapp; **74** AA/J Nicholson; **74/75** AA/J Nicholson; **76** AA/M Lynch; **76/77** AA/C Sawyer; **77** AA/C Sawyer; **78t** AA/C Sawyer; **78b** AA/M Lynch; **79** AA/J Nicholson; **80** AA/C Sawyer; **81** AA/C Sawyer; **82** Photodisc; **83** Digital Vision; **84** Brand X Pictures; **85** AA/C Coe; **88l** AA/M Lynch; **88/89t** AA/M Lynch; **88/89b** AA/M Lynch; **89t** AA/C Coe; **89bl** AA/C Sawyer; **89br** AA/M Lynch; **90** Eric Fowke/Alamy; **91l** AA/C Sawyer; **91r** AA/C Sawyer; **92t** AA/C Sawyer; **92bl** AA/M Lynch; **92br** AA/J Nicholson; **93** AA/J Nicholson; **94** AA/J Tims; **95** AA/C Sawyer; **96** Brand X Pictures; **97t** Photodisc; **97c** AA/D Clapp; **98** AA/T Souter; **99** AA/M Lynch; **102** Photolibrary; **103l** Courtesy of Kennedy Presidential Library Museum; **103r** Courtesy of Kennedy Presidential Library Museum; **104t** AA/C Sawyer; **104b** AA/C Sawyer; **105** AA/P Bennett; **106t** AA/P Bennett; 106bl AA/J Lynch; **106bcl** AA/C Coe; **106bc** AA/C Coe; **106bcr** AA/C Sawyer; **106br** AA/J Lynch; **107** AA/C Sawyer; **108t** AA/C Sawyer; **108ct** AA/M Lynch; **108c** AA/C Sawyer; **108cb** AA/S McBride; **108b** AA/C Sawyer; **109** AA/C Sawyer; **110** AA/C Sawyer; **111** AA/C Sawyer; **112** AA/C Sawyer; **113** AA/C Sawyer; **114** AA/C Coe; **115** AA/C Coe; **116** AA/C Coe; **117** AA/C Coe; **118** AA/C Coe; **119t** AA/C Coe; **119b** AA/C Coe; **120** AA/C Coe; **121t** AA/C Coe; **121b** AA/M Lynch; **122** AA/C Coe; **123** AA/C Coe; **124t** AA/C Coe; **124bl** AA/J Lynch; **124br** AA/C Sawyer; **125t** AA/C Coe; **125bl** AA/C Coe; **125bc** AA/C Sawyer; **125br** AA/C Sawyer

Every effort has been made to trace the copyright holders, and we apologize in advance for any unintentional omissions or errors. We would be pleased to apply any corrections in any following edition of this publication.